Researc

Research Proposals

A practical guide

Martyn Denscombe

 Open University Press

Open University Press
McGraw-Hill Education
McGraw-Hill House
Shoppenhangers Road
Maidenhead
Berkshire
England
SL6 2QL

email: enquiries@openup.co.uk
world wide web: www.openup.co.uk

First published 2012

A catalogue record of this book is available from the British Library

ISBN-13: 978-0-33-524406-5 (pb)
ISBN-10: 0-33-524406-8 (pb)
eISBN: 978-0-33-524407-2

Library of Congress Cataloging-in-Publication Data
CIP data applied for

Typesetting and e-book compilations by
RefineCatch Limited, Bungay, Suffolk
Printed and bound by CPI Group (UK) Ltd, Croydon, CR0 4YY

The **McGraw·Hill** Companies

Overview

Introduction   1

PART 1   WHAT IS A GOOD RESEARCH PROPOSAL?   3

1   Logic and structure of research proposals   5
2   Successful research proposals: two basic criteria   16
3   Selling an idea   32

PART 2   HOW DO I PRODUCE A GOOD RESEARCH PROPOSAL?   43

4   Aims of the research: *What is it all about?*   45
5   Literature review: *What do we already know?*   56
6   Research questions: *What do we need to find out?*   72
7   Research methods: *How will we get the necessary information?*   91
8   Planning and resources: *How long will it take and how much will it cost?*   109
9   Research ethics: *Is the research socially acceptable?*   121
10   Research outcomes: *What will be the benefits?*   137

Appendix 1: Checklist for the submission of a research proposal   144
Appendix 2: Specimen research proposal   146
Appendix 3: Headings and sections in a research proposal   158
Appendix 4: Choosing a research topic   164

References   173
Index   176

Contents

List of figures and tables   xiii

Introduction   1

PART I   WHAT IS A GOOD RESEARCH PROPOSAL?   3

1   THE LOGIC AND STRUCTURE OF RESEARCH PROPOSALS   5

What is a research proposal?   5
Seven basic questions   6
The structure of research proposals   9
The evaluation of research proposals   10
Who approves research proposals?   11
What happens to a research proposal once it is submitted?   12
Summary of key points   14
Further reading   15

2   SUCCESSFUL RESEARCH PROPOSALS   16

Worthwhile research   16
Feasible research   19
The essential elements of a research proposal   22
Why do some research proposals get rejected?   24
Distinctive proposals – what will make a proposal stand
        out from the rest?   25
Summary of key points   30
Further reading   31

3   SELLING AN IDEA   32

Advertising a product   32
Providing information   33
Target audience   35
Value of good timing   36
Art of persuasion   36
Telling the truth   38

Unique selling point 39
Sales pitch 39
Summary of key points 40
Further reading 42

PART II HOW DO I PRODUCE A GOOD RESEARCH PROPOSAL? 43

4 AIMS OF THE RESEARCH 45

Title 46
Keywords 48
Aims 49
Background 51
Summary of key points 54
Further reading 55

5 LITERATURE REVIEW 56

What literature should be included? 57
Literature search 59
What if nothing has been written on the topic? 61
How do I 'review' the publications? 62
An iterative process 65
What message should the literature review contain? 65
Delimitations and scoping the research 69
Summary of key points 70
Further reading 71

6 RESEARCH QUESTIONS 72

The importance of good research questions 73
The format of research questions 74
Types of research question 78
The differences between aims, research problems,
    objectives, and research questions 82
Narrowing the focus: the process of formulating a
    research question 83
The need for an open-minded approach 86
Example 87
Summary of key points 89
Further reading 90

7 RESEARCH METHODS 91

Description of the methods 92
Justification of the choice of methods 101

Risk assessment 103
Limitations 105
Summary of key points 107
Further reading 108

8 PLANNING AND RESOURCES 109

Planning the time 110
The scale of the project 111
Accounting for the costs 114
Researcher skills 118
Summary of key points 118
Further reading 120

9 RESEARCH ETHICS 121

What kinds of research need ethical approval? 122
Do all research proposals need to cover research ethics? 124
Which section of a proposal deals with research ethics? 125
Codes of research ethics 125
Principles of research ethics 128
Risk assessment 131
Ethics approval 132
What are evaluators looking for in the proposal? 133
Summary of key points 135
Further reading 136

10 RESEARCH OUTCOMES 137

Value for money 138
Outcomes and findings 138
Types of outcomes 139
Dissemination of findings 141
Impact 142
Summary of key points 142
Further reading 143

Appendix 1: Checklist for the submission of a research proposal 144
Appendix 2: Specimen research proposal 146
Appendix 3: Headings and sections in a research proposal 158
Appendix 4: Choosing a research topic 164

References 173
Index 176

List of figures and tables

FIGURE 1.1 The logic of research proposals 6
FIGURE 2.1 The essential elements of a research proposal 23
FIGURE 5.1 The Literature Review: an iterative process 65
FIGURE 6.1 Narrowing the focus of research 83
FIGURE 6.2 The iterative process of formulating research questions 84
FIGURE 6.3 Developing research questions – narrowing the focus 85
FIGURE 8.1 Time planning and scheduling for research 112
FIGURE A.1 Narrowing the topic: an example 170

TABLE 1.1 The structure of research proposals 9
TABLE 1.2 The evaluation of research proposals 11
TABLE 2.1 Common reasons for the rejection of proposals 24
TABLE 3.1 Targeting the research proposal: right time, right place 36
TABLE 3.2 Research proposals: an advertisement for a research idea 41
TABLE 5.1 Literature of relevance to a research topic 62
TABLE 6.1 Research questions – an example 88
TABLE A.1 Topics that can and cannot be researched 167

INTRODUCTION

The basic aims of a research proposal are not complicated, and anyone who needs to produce a research proposal will have a much simpler task if they constantly bear in mind just three core things.

First, research proposals need to persuade their audience that the proposed research will be *worthwhile*. The proposal needs to show that there are some clear and obvious benefits to be gained from undertaking the investigation. The specific kinds of things that will qualify as being worthwhile will vary according to the particular audience that is being addressed but the task for the writer of a proposal is always to demonstrate that there is

- some *need* for the research.

Second, research proposals must convince their audience that the proposed research is *feasible*. It is not sufficient just to have a good research idea: that idea needs to be something that can be accomplished and delivered on time. It needs to be realistic. It must not be over-ambitious in its aims and must not promise to do things that are unlikely to be achieved on the basis of:

- the available time and resources;
- access to data;
- the researcher's experience and expertise;
- ethical, legal, environmental, and safety issues.

The third thing to bear in mind is that research proposals involve *selling an idea*. The success of the proposal will depend in large part on how good it is at communicating the purpose of the research and persuading the audience about the value of the proposed research. This means it needs to be effective in the way it:

- *communicates* its ideas to a specific *target audience;*
- manages to *persuade* them that the proposed research warrants support.

> Good research proposals persuade the reader that a proposed piece of research is both worthwhile and feasible. This simple and straightforward premise applies to all kinds of research proposals.

This book develops these themes and provides practical advice on how to produce a successful research proposal. It does not presume any previous experience of conducting research projects, and does not rely on any familiarity with particular research techniques or methodologies. In clear language and straightforward terms, it describes what needs to be included in a research proposal and explains why this is the case.

The guidance provided by this book is relevant for a wide range of situations where research proposals are required. This is because research proposals produced for different kinds of research, in different disciplines, across different continents, tend to have a lot in common in terms of their basic aims and their structure. It is easy to see a similarity in proposals written for research in the social sciences, the natural sciences, the humanities and the arts, and proposals linked to funding for large-scale research with huge budgets will share much with proposals written for small-scale research using minimal resources.

That having been said, this book is geared primarily to the needs of *social science* students – those who need to undertake research in areas such as business studies, education, health studies, media studies, marketing, politics, sociology, economics, and psychology. And it focuses on the needs of students who are required to undertake a *small-scale* research project that involves *empirical data* collection. It is particularly useful in this respect for those who need to write a research proposal for:

- a bachelor's degree project;
- a master's degree dissertation;
- an application for acceptance onto a PhD programme.

I

WHAT IS A GOOD RESEARCH PROPOSAL?

1

THE LOGIC AND STRUCTURE OF RESEARCH PROPOSALS

• What is a research proposal? • Seven basic questions • The structure of research proposals • The evaluation of research proposals • Who approves research proposals? • What happens to a research proposal once it is submitted? • Summary of key points • Further reading

What is a research proposal?

A research proposal is a relatively brief document that contains an outline plan for a research project. It is produced at the beginning of the research process in advance of any data collection. A well-constructed research proposal offers a blueprint for the research that shows what the parts look like and how they will fit together. It describes what will be done, explains how it will be done, and justifies why the research should be undertaken.

A research proposal is an important part of the research process because the success of any project depends on forward planning and organization. A good proposal is based on careful thought about how the project will be conducted and involves the kind of advance planning that is required if a project is to run smoothly. There is a useful analogy here with house building. No-one would seriously consider starting work on a house without first having drawn up plans for the building. Without such plans it would be virtually impossible to work out exactly what materials will be required, when they are to be delivered, and how they will fit together. The same applies with a research project. Before embarking on a research project, the researcher needs to prepare the groundwork and give careful thought to the practical issues involved at the implementation stage of the research.

Seven basic questions

There is logic to research proposals, and it is really very simple. It can be expressed as a sequence of *seven basic questions* that it is reasonable to ask about any proposed research (see Figure 1.1). These questions reflect a general

FIGURE 1.1 The logic of research proposals

way of thinking about research and are the ones that most readers will have in their minds when they consider whether a proposal is worthwhile and whether it is feasible. Of course, the sophistication of the answers provided to these questions will vary according to the circumstances; much will depend on the purpose of the proposal and the level of expertise expected of the researcher. Successful proposals, however, have this in common: they manage to address the seven questions in a way that satisfies the requirements of their particular audience.

Question 1: What is it all about?

This is a fundamental question that readers will ask about any research proposal. First and foremost, they will want to know what the topic is and they will be looking for precise information about the subject matter of the research. And they are also entitled to ask what the research is trying to accomplish. What is the purpose of the research and what is it trying to achieve? Without this information the readers of the research proposal cannot evaluate the proposal. They cannot judge whether the methodology is appropriate or whether there will be sufficient time and resources to complete the project. And they will get frustrated and annoyed if they do not get this information supplied clearly, precisely, and succinctly in the proposal.

Question 2: What do we already know about the subject?

Having addressed the question of what the research is all about, the next logical thing that readers of a proposal will ask is: What do we already know about the subject? What has previous research revealed and where have we got to in terms of our knowledge about the topic? This is a relevant and important question to pose in this context. Primarily, this is because a review of the existing information can prevent us from undertaking research that is not necessary. There is no point in 'reinventing the wheel'. If the information already exists, there is no point in repeating the research (unless we have the specific aim of checking the validity of the earlier findings).

Question 3: What does the research need to find out?

Once readers are clear about the aims of the research and what is already known about the topic, the next step logically is for them to ask what *new* information is needed. A review of the existing information not only tells us what we already know, it tells us what we don't know and what it would be useful to find out. This allows the proposed research to be targeted where it will be most useful. It helps to pinpoint the kind of things that need to be studied to shed some light on the topic – the factors (variables, indicators, relationships, etc.) that it will prove useful to focus upon if the research is to produce findings that are relevant in terms of saying anything new or useful about the topic of research. Readers will be looking for these things to be spelled out clearly and precisely, usually in the form of 'research questions'.

Question 4: How will we get the necessary information?

Having established precisely what the research needs to find out, the next question is fairly obvious: How will the necessary information be obtained? A description of the research methods is called for in order to answer this question. Proposals always include an account of how the researcher intends to collect the data, how much data will be collected, and what techniques will be used to analyse the data. Armed with such information readers can draw their own conclusions about whether the methods are suitable or not for the task at hand, and whether or not the proposed methods are likely to work in practice. It is these kind of judgements, of course, that are crucial when it comes to deciding whether a proposal appears to be worthwhile and feasible, and ultimately whether it is successful or not.

Question 5: What will it cost and how long will it take?

Research takes time and costs money, and this is something that readers of research proposals will recognize. It will be of concern to them in terms of the feasibility of the proposed project. They will want to know what resources are necessary for the successful completion of the research, and they will be looking for evidence within the proposal that the researcher has planned the research in accord with the amount of time that is available and the amount of money at his or her disposal for the completion of the project.

Question 6: Is the research socially acceptable?

Readers will want to feel assured that the proposed research will be conducted in a manner that meets socially accepted standards governing research activity. They will realize that if there are any doubts on this point it is almost certain that the research project will not be allowed to proceed. Mindful of this, they will look for guarantees that the research will be conducted in a manner that abides by the principles of research ethics and accords with the law of the land.

Question 7: What are the benefits?

Most readers will expect a piece of research to be justified on the basis that it will produce some specific, identifiable benefits. Indeed, it is rarely the case that research can be justified 'for its own sake'. For this reason, it is important for research proposals to address questions about the outcomes of the research and the end-products that it is hoped will arise from the research. They need to contain a clear account of the 'deliverables' from the project and an explanation of who, or what, might benefit as a direct result of the project.

The structure of research proposals

As Table 1.1 indicates, these seven questions provide a rationale for the way that research proposals are organized. They provide a basis for providing the readership with relevant information – allowing the vital material to be presented in an efficient manner, in a format that is familiar and a sequence that allows readers to understand things quickly, easily, and with the minimum of effort.

The headings listed in Table 1.1 can be used as the basis for writing a research proposal. They will be recognizable to readers from a wide range of research backgrounds and they provide a sound, generic framework for organizing all the relevant material.

However, we need to be a little cautious about treating them like a 'one-size-fits-all' form that can be pulled off the shelf and used in connection with any research proposal in any context. One reason for this is that the kind of detail that is required in a proposal can vary according to the nature of the subject area of the research. It is easy to understand that proposals might look slightly different if they are written to suit the nature of research in particular areas, especially when those areas are as diverse as business, engineering, medicine, sociology, education, history, languages, and so on.

Another reason is that various agencies and organizations that receive research proposals often produce bespoke forms with their own headings to suit their own purposes. They are at liberty to do so and there is no single body with the authority to enforce the use of one single model of a standard research proposal form. This means that when it comes to writing a research proposal, the first thing that a researcher must do is check whether his or her proposal needs to be submitted using a particular form or needs to adhere to specific guidelines provided by the body to which the proposal will be

Table 1.1 The structure of research proposals

Typical headings/sections	Basic questions	Guidance in this book
Title Keywords Aims Background	What is it all about?	Chapter 4
Literature review	What do we already know?	Chapter 5
Research questions	What do we need to find out?	Chapter 6
Methods	How will we get the necessary information?	Chapter 7
Planning and resources	How long will it take and what will it cost?	Chapter 8
Ethics	Is the research socially acceptable?	Chapter 9
Outcomes	What will be the benefits?	Chapter 10

submitted. If so, then there is no option but to use the headings and sections as supplied. This is an absolute must. Any attempt to change the stipulated headings and sections is likely to jeopardize the proposal's prospects of success.

Top tip
Always use the prescribed format when one is available.

Although 'No universally applicable and correct format exists for the research proposal' (Locke et al. 2000: 7), there is still a *strong family resemblance* underlying the structure and headings to be found across the whole spectrum of disciplines and organizations involved. This, as we have noted, reflects the seven questions that can be asked about any research project. There is a shared logic to the many alternatives and, as Appendix 3 shows, this results in a familiar feel to the headings and sections adopted across a range of approaches and different research traditions.

The evaluation of research proposals

Most research projects need to gain approval from a relevant authority before they are allowed to start and the research proposal provides the kind of vital information that enables relevant authorities to evaluate the research and make a decision about whether to approve/support the work and allow it to go ahead.

The analogy with house building is again useful on this point. No reasonable person would start the construction of a house without having sought permission from relevant authorities to embark on the construction. Plans have to be drawn up to show that the house will be structurally sound and that it will meet all the necessary requirements in terms of building regulations. Well, the same logic applies to a research project. In the same way that there are regulations and procedures that are designed to protect the public from rogue builders constructing houses that are likely to collapse or which fail to meet environmental standards, there are standards and procedures that researchers need to take into account to avoid poor research designs that are likely to fail. The blueprint for research contained in research proposals provides the kind of information that allows people to check whether the proposed research will accord with the necessary procedures and regulations and it thus allows those who authorize research to make judgements about the quality of the proposed investigation and the likelihood that it will work and that it will have some beneficial outcomes.

The point to remember, then, is that research proposals are essentially documents that will be *evaluated*. They are written for a purpose, and that purpose is invariably connected with getting approval for the plan of research that is contained in the proposal. Proposals are written with a view to being evaluated by individuals or committees who have the authority to allow the research to go ahead, or to prevent it from taking place. This applies whether the proposal is written for an undergraduate research project, a master's degree dissertation or an application for entry to a doctoral research programme. And it also applies when proposals are written as part of a bid for funding or as part of an application for ethics approval. All proposals are scrutinized by experts who use their experience to make judgements about the quality of what is being proposed and the prospects that it can be delivered. Successful research proposals recognize this point. They are produced with a constant eye on the evaluators – who they will be, what they will expect, and what will ignite their enthusiasm.

> By their nature, research proposals are documents that are *evaluated* by their readers.

Who approves research proposals?

Broadly speaking, approval can take four different forms (see Table 1.2). Proposals linked to master's dissertations and bachelor's degree projects are generally submitted to tutors who will act as supervisors to the students during

Table 1.2 The evaluation of research proposals

Purpose of the proposal	People who evaluate the proposal
Approval for research project on a degree programme	
• master's dissertation	Supervisors
• undergraduate project	Tutors
Applications for acceptance onto a research degree programme	
• PhD application	Research committees, potential supervisors
Funding applications	
• research grant	Review panels, subject experts
Ethics approval	Human research ethics committees, Institutional review boards (USA)

their relatively short-term research project. These people will be concerned with whether the research is likely to prove worthwhile in terms of knowledge in the subject area, but they will also want to be assured that the proposed research is possible within the resource constraints and the tight time constraints within which dissertations and projects need to be completed.

When a proposal is submitted as part of an application for acceptance onto a PhD programme, the people who evaluate the proposal will be potential PhD supervisors or members of committees established to ensure that entrants on a PhD programme will be embarking on a worthwhile piece of research and that the applicant is academically good enough to take on the task. In this case, the evaluators will place high priority on the potential contribution of the research in terms of advancing theory or solving a significant practical problem.

If the proposal has been produced to gain funding for the research, the funding body will nominate who is to evaluate it. They are likely to be experts who are very knowledgeable about what research already exists in the area. They will have a particular eye on the quality of the research design and the potential value of findings from the proposed research, and will be looking for 'cutting-edge' research that can advance knowledge in that particular field of study.

Proposals that are submitted to gain ethical approval are reviewed by committees (or sometimes individuals) with a specific remit to ensure that the research is properly conducted and incorporates appropriate measures to protect the interests of those who will be called upon to participate in the research.

What happens to a research proposal once it is submitted?

Once a research proposal is submitted, the process by which it is evaluated will depend on the purpose of the proposal and on the organization that is involved. Funders, admissions tutors, supervisors, and ethics committees will differ in how formal their systems are and how many stages are involved in the approval process.

In the case of bachelor's degree projects and master's degree dissertations, the procedures for approval are not likely to include the formal review process outlined below. In practice, the 'review' will probably be undertaken by the project supervisor, without the involvement of administrators or committees in the process.

However, in the case of funding, admissions to university programmes, and ethics approval, the systems are likely to be quite formal and, in such cases, the organizations concerned will normally be quite explicit about their approval system. It should be relatively easy to find out exactly what will happen to such proposals; details will either be given on the application form itself or will be available on the organization's website. In general, however, the process is likely to involve the following stages:

Stage 1: Check and process

Where formal systems operate to evaluate research proposals, they will generally follow a path that starts with an initial check of the proposal to ensure that it meets the stipulated requirements and that it is eligible for consideration. The application is likely to be checked in the first instance by *administrators*. Their role is to check that the proposal is complete and that it meets the conditions, the layout, and remit that have been laid down. The administrators will check that the necessary signatures have been included on the forms (or electronic equivalents), that essential information has been supplied, and that the proposal has not exceeded the word limit.

> The Economic and Social Research Council in the UK estimates that 10 per cent of bids for funding are rejected immediately because they have not been produced in accord with the guidelines set out.

Stage 2: Review and evaluate

The proposal will be sent to relevant experts who will be asked to review and comment upon the quality of the proposal. These 'referees' are selected not only on the basis of their subject expertise but also as being able to offer an impartial and unbiased view on the project. Sometimes the person or team submitting the proposal can nominate one of more of the referees to be used, but in most cases the reviewing process will involve referees who are chosen by the organization. As the applicant, you do not normally get to know the identity of the independent experts who evaluate your proposal.

Stage 3: Selection and decision

The views of the referees are collected and a *decision* is then made either by a specific individual or by a committee. This process can take some time, particularly if the decision is to be made by a committee who are scheduled to meet periodically. Details of the frequency of meetings and the dates on which decisions are notified to applicants should be part of the information that accompanies any application process – either in paper format or online at the organization's website. If in doubt, the administrators can be contacted to supply the dates.

If the *selection* process is competitive, only a few proposals will be successful among the many submitted. This is especially the case for funding applications where the selection process can sometimes involve a number of stages. The early stages involve sifting out projects that are seen to have little chance of success. There might be obvious question marks against aspects of the proposal, which mean it needs to be eliminated. A process of short-listing progressively reduces the number of proposals until the final decisions are made.

Stage 4: Feedback

The decision, together with *feedback* in the form of referees' comments, is sent to the applicant. If the proposal is accepted outright, break open a bottle of champagne! However, the referees often request amendments to, or development of, a proposal. And, unfortunately, many proposals are rejected outright. In either of the latter instances, the feedback that accompanies the decision can be painful for the applicant. First reactions might well be that the feedback involves unfair criticism and a misunderstanding of what was said in the proposal. However, before dismissing the feedback, it is wise to pause for a while and then look for the lessons to be learned and the constructive things than can be gleaned from the feedback because there is generally good advice in there somewhere.

Stage 5: Appeal

If the research proposal is rejected, there may, or may not, be a process of *appeal* against the decision. This will have been made clear in the documentation about the application. In reality, though, even if there is a process of appeal, it is unlikely to lead to a reversal of the original decision.

Summary of key points

Research proposals contain a brief plan for a research project that describes the purpose of the research and how it will be conducted. For the researcher who has produced the proposal, this represents the outcome of a planning exercise in which attention will have been given to fine-tuning the aims of the research and working out how best to conduct the investigation. It involves the kind of planning and forethought that are necessary to enable the project to run smoothly.

Research proposals serve an equally if not more important purpose as well. A brief summary of what will be done and why it will be done provides the basis upon which readers can arrive at judgements about the quality of the research that is being proposed. Crucial among these readers are the individuals or committees to whom the proposal is submitted who are in a position to approve the project and allow the research to proceed or who can reject the proposal and effectively prevent the work from taking place. Success depends on their verdict.

The process of evaluation sometimes allows resubmission of a proposal if in the first instance it is not approved. At other times, there is no possibility of resubmitting. Either way, the sensible approach is to ensure that the proposal is 'right first time' – that it addresses all of the key concerns that evaluators might have.

As we have seen, these key concerns centre around *seven basic questions* – questions that can be applied to practically any piece of research. These are straightforward questions that the people who evaluate research proposals, whatever their research tradition or academic discipline, are almost certain to ask about any proposed research. Although there is no simple template for the structure of a research proposal that operates in all circumstances, the contents and structure of research proposals generally tend to follow the logic of these seven questions.

Further reading

Krathwohl, D.R. and Smith, N.L. (2005) *How to Prepare a Dissertation Proposal: Suggestions for Students in Education and the Social and Behavioral Sciences*. Syracuse, NY: Syracuse University Press (Chapters 1–3).

Locke, L.F., Spirduso, W.W. and Silverman, S.J. (2007) *Proposals that Work: A Guide for Planning Dissertations and Grant Proposals* (5th edn.). Thousand Oaks, CA: Sage (Chapter 1).

Punch, K. (2006) *Developing Effective Research Proposals* (2nd edn.). Thousand Oaks, CA: Sage (Chapter 2).

2

SUCCESSFUL RESEARCH PROPOSALS

• Worthwhile research • Feasible research • The essential elements of a research proposal • Why do some research proposals get rejected? • Distinctive proposals – what will make a proposal stand out from the rest? • Summary of key points • Further reading

---

The people who evaluate research proposals are basically concerned with two things only: First, does the proposal convince them that the research is a good idea – is it *worthwhile*? Second, does the proposal appear to be do-able in a practical sense – is it *feasible*? To be successful, a research proposal needs to develop an argument that persuades the readers that the answer is 'yes' to both questions.

Worthwhile research

Research needs to be 'worthwhile' because it takes time and money to undertake and the evaluators will believe, quite reasonably, that resources should not be wasted on activities that are unlikely to produce results of any real value. This would be a waste of the researchers' time and, perhaps more importantly, a waste of participants' time, if they have volunteered to assist the researchers with their project.

Any research proposal needs to recognize this point. It has to address the issue head-on and persuade the reader that the topic of the investigation is something that matters and that the research is likely to produce some clear and specific benefits. Proposals need to pre-empt questions about the value of conducting the research and they need to make a strong case built around what is to be gained from the research and who will benefit from it.

> Research activity is not a frivolous pastime – it is not undertaken on a whim or done just for fun. To qualify as genuine research, it must be directed towards something positive and have a clear purpose from which benefits can arise.

A need for the research

The most obvious way to convince readers that a piece of research is worthwhile is to pinpoint the *need* for the research. The research, in a figure of speech, should 'scratch where it itches', and what the proposal should do is demonstrate precisely what the 'itch' is and precisely how the 'scratch' will deal with the 'itch'. This is where the *literature review* section of a research proposal comes into play, providing the opportunity to convince evaluators that there is a definite need for the new research outlined in the proposal.

Link up with **Chapter 5: Literature Review**

This point deserves a little elaboration. It might appear that by concentrating on 'needs', and the ability of specific research projects to meet those needs, we might be adopting a very pragmatic stance on research. It might be argued that this does not allow for 'blue-skies' thinking or enquiries based on moments of inspiration. Why should research always be constrained by what fits today's agenda – what we know already and practical problems that already exist? Surely this simply ties all research to a single path constrained by the past, without allowing research to explore off-the-wall ideas and develop genuinely novel directions in thinking? Certainly, there is some validity to such points (for a classic treatise on this topic, see Feyerabend 1993). However, for small-scale social research projects undertaken by relative beginners, the rules of the game will almost certainly involve the need to relate the proposed research to existing, clearly identified needs. Whatever the merits of the 'blue-skies' approach, it does not accord with the prevailing sentiment governing the evaluation of research proposals. The only sound advice, therefore, is to ensure that your research proposal somehow ties in with existing needs and that the reader can clearly see what those are.

Top tip
Worthwhile research addresses specific needs.

Benefits from the research

People who evaluate proposals will want to know what the likely benefits are. Is anything likely to arise from the proposed research that might be valuable and which warrants the use of people's time and the organization's money to investigate? In their minds, they will be asking how the research will take things forward and they will expect to find in the proposal explicit statements about how the research will make a difference.

To address that question, the proposal should indicate what the *outcomes* of the research are anticipated to be. This is not to be confused with trying to state what the findings will be; the findings are something that can only be stated once the research has been completed. The outcomes, however, can be identified in advance because they concern the kind of 'deliverables' that researchers see as the end-product of their research activity. These can include things like:

- a contribution to knowledge;
- the development of good practice;
- the dissemination and impact of findings.

Within the research proposal, the *deliverables* can be listed in a section under the heading 'Outcomes'. Many research proposal forms include such a heading, and highlight the importance of providing such information. Even if there is no specific 'outcomes' heading in the proposal form, it is important to ensure that those who are to evaluate the proposal have a clear picture of what will be produced by the research, thus making it 'value for money'.

Link up with **Chapter 10: Research Outcomes**

> **Top tip**
>
> Be clear about the outcomes from the research. Specify what will be produced and what will be the benefits arising from the study.

Use of suitable methods

If research is to be worthwhile, it needs to use suitable methods. If it is a good topic but it is researched poorly, then it will be of little value. At best the findings will be not as good as they could have been; at worst the findings could be misleading or useless. For this reason, evaluators will scrutinize the proposal to check that the data collection procedures and the data analysis techniques are suitable.

> A good topic poorly researched is of little value.

Whether or not the methods are suitable depends on the match between *what* the research is trying to find out and *how* it is intended to do this. Within a proposal, the 'research questions' are crucial in this respect because they pinpoint exactly what it is that the research will be looking at. Proposals are expected to be clear on this score. The research methods that are chosen can then be judged in terms of how good, or perhaps how poor, they are likely to be when it comes to producing findings that directly answer those questions. But, of course, this can only be done if the proposal also contains sufficient information about what data will be collected, how the data will be collected, and how the data will be analysed.

Link up with **Chapter 6: Research Questions**

Link up with **Chapter 7: Research Methods**

Feasible research

No matter how good an idea for research might be in principle, it will not provide the foundation for a successful research proposal unless it can be put into practice. Evaluators will be thinking: 'Nice idea – but can you actually do it?', and they will need to be persuaded that the proposed research is indeed feasible. They will pose the questions: Will the research meet its objectives? What are the chances of success or failure? Can the research be done and, equally, can it be done *properly*? Certainly, they will not 'buy into' an idea if they feel that there is little chance of the investigation being successful. So, within the proposal it is the researcher's responsibility to make the case that the research is possible in real terms – that there is a real chance of it achieving its aims. This involves addressing any doubts the readers might have in relation to the following four things:

- the scope and scale of the research
- access to data sources
- available resources
- ethics

The scope and scale of the research

Research proposals should never promise outcomes that cannot be delivered. There is a danger, however, that in the effort to impress the readers the proposal might actually aim too high and become over-ambitious. This can backfire and have the opposite effect because promising too much may be considered a weakness by those evaluating the research. What it does is to reveal a certain inexperience or naivety on the part of the researcher. In practice, the readers of the proposal will be far more impressed by a submission that has a relatively narrow focus but which looks as though it can be investigated reasonably within the time scale and using the money that is available.

Link up with **Chapter 4: Aims of the Research**

Link up with **Chapter 8: Planning and Resources**

> **Top tip**
> Do not 'bite off more than you can chew'. Focus upon a topic that is sufficiently narrow that it can be completed using the resources that are available.

Access to data sources

The feasibility of research hinges on gaining access to the necessary data sources; if this is not possible, or even if it is seen as problematic, it represents a major stumbling block for the proposal. Researchers must be certain that they can gain access to the kind of data necessary to investigate the proposed topic. If there is any doubt about this, the proposal is unlikely to be successful.

This is one of the most fundamental concerns of anyone evaluating a research proposal; indeed, there is a case for saying that it is the most important consideration when it comes to the feasibility of a project. If you cannot collect the necessary data, the project is doomed to failure. Thus within the proposal, the researcher needs to provide some assurances that obtaining access to the people, the situations, the events, the databases, etc., that are necessary for the research will not be a problem.

Link up with **Chapter 7: Research Methods**

Available resources

Research occurs within constraints imposed by the available resources to complete it. Time and money are factors that cannot be ignored and, as we have seen, the scope and scale of the proposed project need to be in balance with the resources available. So, when evaluators look at a proposal they will ask themselves: 'Can the research be done properly with the resources that are available?' They will want to be confident that the research project is based on a time and money budget that can be met, and that the researcher is not being unrealistically optimistic about what can be accomplished.

The time scale for delivery of the work will come as a 'given' in most cases. Whether the proposal is written as part of a funding application or for a bachelor's project, master's dissertation or PhD thesis, there is generally a quite specific deadline that has to be adhered to. What evaluators will look for in this regard is some evidence of planning for completion on time. They will want to see some schedule for conducting the various parts of the research, perhaps in the form of a Gantt chart.

The costs involved in the project should also be considered within the proposal, although the amount of detail on this will depend on the purpose for which the proposal has been written. When proposals form part of an application for funding, considerable detail is likely to be required. Details about salaries, travel, and other significant items of expenditure will be expected. In the case of proposals for bachelor's projects, master's dissertations or PhD theses, there is generally less demand for such details. It is implicit that costs are quite small, that the researcher's time comes for free as part of the study for the academic award, and that overheads will be covered by the institution.

Link up with **Chapter 8: Planning and Resources**

Top tip
State what resources are needed and confirm that they are available.

Ethics

The success of a proposal is built on the presumption that the research can be conducted without putting anyone in 'harm's way'. It depends on the proposal being able to confirm, with some certainty, that the research can be completed without infringing the rights of the people involved, without jeopardizing their safety or well-being, and without breaking the law. Evaluators of research proposals will have such matters to the front of their minds when judging whether a proposal is feasible, and they will want to be convinced from reading the proposal that the nature of the proposed research does not violate ethical principles and that there are no other legal or safety issues likely to be thrown up by the research that will make it unacceptable. To this end, they will look within the proposal for a *risk assessment* by the researcher, which anticipates significant problems that might occur and which incorporates measures that can avoid these risks or minimize the impact of such risks.

As part of this concern, evaluators will look at the skills and experience that the researcher brings to the project. On practical grounds, they know that a research project is unlikely to succeed if the researcher overstretches his or her abilities or attempts to use techniques for which he or she does not have the necessary training or skills. Equally, from an ethical point of view, they will need to feel that the researcher has the *competence* to undertake the research without wasting people's time or exposing them to unnecessary risks.

Link up with **Chapter 9: Research Ethics**

> Research that is not ethical is not acceptable, and research that is not acceptable is not feasible.

The essential elements of a research proposal

At the start of this chapter the point was made that research proposals need to address two basic questions: is the research worthwhile and is it feasible? Subsequently, the factors that will persuade readers on these two questions have been briefly outlined so that we can get an overview of what is entailed in a successful research proposal. This overview is depicted in Figure 2.1, which provides a vision of the issues and concerns that need to be discussed within a proposal and the reasons why they need to be included. As well as showing what the elements of a research proposal are, Figure 2.1 also acts as a road map, pointing to where these elements of research proposals are considered in greater depth in later parts of the book.

FIGURE 2.1 The essential elements of a research proposal

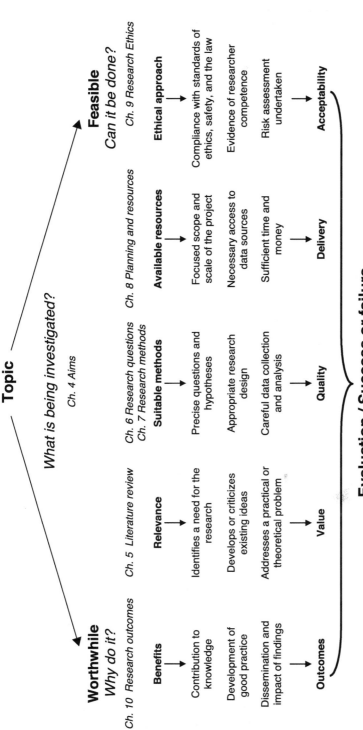

Topic

What is being investigated?

Worthwhile
Why do it?

Feasible
Can it be done?

Ch. 10 Research outcomes | Ch. 5 Literature review | Ch. 6 Research questions | Ch. 8 Planning and resources | Ch. 9 Research Ethics
Ch. 7 Research methods

Ch. 4 Aims

Benefits

Contribution to knowledge

Development of good practice

Dissemination and impact of findings

Outcomes

Relevance

Identifies a need for the research

Develops or criticizes existing ideas

Addresses a practical or theoretical problem

Value

Suitable methods

Precise questions and hypotheses

Appropriate research design

Careful data collection and analysis

Quality

Available resources

Focused scope and scale of the project

Necessary access to data sources

Sufficient time and money

Delivery

Ethical approach

Compliance with standards of ethics, safety, and the law

Evidence of researcher competence

Risk assessment undertaken

Acceptability

Evaluation / Success or failure

© M.Denscombe. Research Proposals.
Maidenhead: McGraw-Hill 2012

Why do some research proposals get rejected?

Proposals that contain weaknesses are liable to be rejected. Indeed, a large percentage of proposals that are rejected suffer from significant omissions or errors, or have been sent to the wrong place. This is frustrating for those who have the task of evaluating the proposals and, in response, a number of experts have set about cataloguing the main causes of failed proposals (see Table 2.1). This might seem a rather depressing thing to do, but their motive is to flag up the common areas of weakness in research proposals so that people can learn from the mistakes of others. As experienced evaluators of research proposals they see the same kind of error or weakness repeated time and again, and by pointing to these weaknesses they hope others will be able to avoid them, and thus the quality of proposals will improve.

Unfortunately, there is another message that comes through from their work. It is a rather stark warning to prospective proposal writers that failure should not be treated as some remote possibility. It should be treated, instead,

Table 2.1 Common reasons for the rejection of proposals

Weaknesses related to the *research problem*:
- The description of the project is so nebulous and unfocused that the purpose of the research is unclear
- The problem is unimportant or unlikely to yield new information
- The hypothesis is ill-defined, doubtful or unsound, or it rests on insufficient evidence
- The problem is more complex than the investigator realizes
- The problem is of interest only to a particular, localized group, or in some other way has limited relevance to the field as a whole

Weaknesses related to the *research design and methodology*:
- The description of the design and/or method is so vague and unfocused as to prevent adequate evaluation of its worth
- The data the investigator wishes to use are either difficult to access or inappropriate for the research problem
- The proposed methods, measurement instruments or procedures are inappropriate for the research problem

Weaknesses related to the *investigator*:
- The investigator does not have sufficient training or experience for the proposed research
- The investigator appears to be unfamiliar with the literature relevant to the research problem
- The investigator does not have sufficient time to devote to the project

Weaknesses related to *resources*:
- The institutional setting is unfavourable for the proposed research
- The proposed use of equipment, support staff or other resources is unrealistic

Source: Based on, and adapted from, a list presented by Leedy and Ormrod (2009) that draws on research by Allen (1960) and Cuca and McLoughlin (1987).

as a very real danger. And it is a danger that can have very serious consequences. Many research proposals take the form of a 'one-off' application and for this reason they need to be 'right first time'. If the proposal forms part of a bid for funding or an application for a place on a PhD programme, it can quite simply be rejected. This is not only painful, it can also be irretrievable; the rejection may not come with a 'second chance' option. And even when the proposal can be improved through a second or possibly third iteration – for example, when submitted in preparation for a master's dissertation or a bachelor's project – receiving critical comments and poor grades for the proposal is to be avoided at all costs.

Rejection, however, is not necessarily the result of submitting a weak proposal. The harsh reality is that some research proposals will get rejected simply because there are not enough places (e.g. applications to a PhD programme) or there is not enough money (e.g. with funding applications). The number of proposals simply outweighs the available resources. This means that some perfectly good research proposals will be rejected – which is a bitter pill to swallow for the researchers involved. The point here, though, is that proposals are often produced in a competitive environment in which evaluators are faced with the task of sifting through many good proposals and selecting just the very best of the bunch. In such cases, being good may not be good enough. Being best is better.

> **Top tip**
> Sometimes, success depends on being 'better than the rest'.

Distinctive proposals – what will make a proposal stand out from the rest?

In a competitive environment, the proposal really needs to contain something that will make it get noticed and stand out above others. It needs to have qualities that make it a particularly attractive proposition – things that not only make it worthwhile but which make it *more* worthwhile than alternative proposals on offer. Bearing this in mind, there are five aspects of a proposal that are particularly important for making the case that the proposed research is more than just worthwhile – it is *very* worthwhile.

Originality

The prospect of doing 'original' research might appear rather daunting, especially to those writing proposals for bachelor's projects and master's dissertations. But it need not be. There is absolutely no reason to panic at the thought that the proposal will be judged on this criterion alone, and there are two reasons for this. First, expectations will differ according to the level of work involved. Although the notion of original research will apply to PhD theses and to funding applications, for bachelor's projects and master's dissertations the expectations will be adjusted to the level of award for which the work is being produced and the limited time scale and resources available for conducting the research. Second, in practice, it is possible to meet this criterion without the need for ground-breaking, advanced research. The notion that the research should contain an element of originality merely means that when choosing the topic for research, attention needs to be paid to what is *different* about the proposed research – what it is that distinguishes it from other investigations on the topic (for further discussion on this point, see Denscombe 2010).

What the proposal needs to do is to demonstrate to the reader that there is some aspect of the research that makes it stand out from previous investigations in the area – something that might lead to a new insight about the topic. In the proposal this can be done by:

- showing evidence of *critical thinking* – rather than a simple rehash of old ideas;
- acknowledging the existence of *alternative views*, competing theories, and counter-information – engaging with ideas or evidence that do not support your own position;
- *avoiding plagiarism* – resisting any temptation to paste chunks of text from the web or other published sources into the proposal; this is relatively easy to detect and will be treated as 'stealing' the work of others.

Originality clearly requires some effort to find out what has already been written on a particular topic so that both the researcher and the audience for the research feel confident that the research is not 'reinventing the wheel'. The element of originality can be flagged up briefly in the 'Aims' section of the proposal but mostly it is within the 'Literature Review' section that the researcher has the opportunity to evaluate the existing research in the area and to argue that what he or she is proposing can make a contribution that is in some way or other new, different, unique – in some way original – and all the more worthwhile for it.

Timeliness

Research proposals that are 'timely' will have an advantage when it comes to persuading evaluators that the research warrants support. They will be seen as more valuable and likely to make more of a contribution to the field than more routine projects based on topics and methods that have been around for some time. Evaluators are looking for something that is 'up-to-date' rather than 'old hat'. They will be impressed by evidence contained within the proposal that the topic is engaging with something that is timely and of current interest. And they will feel more assured about the value of the research where the proposal indicates that the researcher is conversant with the latest thinking on the topic. In essence, proposals will have a competitive advantage when they can persuade the reader that the research will be:

- timely in respect of current issues; and
- based on an awareness of current thinking and positions in the field of study.

As with the matter of originality, though, the prospect of producing a 'cutting-edge' proposal might appear rather daunting. But, as with the matter of originality, there are two things that need to be borne in mind. First, expectations will differ according to the nature of the proposal and who is producing it. Whereas evaluators of proposals for PhD research and for research funding might have this high on their agenda when deciding which proposals should succeed and which should not, evaluators of proposals produced in connection with a bachelor's degree project or master's dissertation are less likely to do so. So, let us be clear, this is not an absolutely vital criterion for the success of *all* research proposals – much will depend on the purpose for which the proposal is being written and the level of expertise expected of the researcher.

Second, there are a couple of fairly basic and straightforward ways in which it is possible to address the matter of the timeliness of the work and the extent to which it represents 'cutting-edge' research. The first is to convey an impression of timeliness by including a few well-chosen *buzzwords* in the proposal. The websites and publications of organizations and individuals who evaluate proposals often emphasize certain terms or concepts that are in vogue and considered pertinent in relation to their current research agenda. Without going to excess, there can be a competitive advantage gained by incorporating a few of these into the proposal. Perhaps more crucially, though, the proposal should always include some *references to recent studies in the field*. It is fine to cite classic studies as a foundation for the proposal but, to complement these, care should taken to ensure that at least some of the sources cited in the proposal have been published in the current or the previous year. The date of publication of such studies acts like a signal to evaluators that the researcher is aware of current thinking and positions on the topic; it conveys a sense that the proposed research is up-to-date. The corollary to this is that any proposal that includes only 'old' references is likely to jeopardize the prospects of success by suggesting to the evaluator that the proposed research is 'off the pace', 'old hat' or 'past its sell-by date'.

Top tip
Show that the proposal is in tune with current thinking.

A topic that is of particular interest – one that 'pushes the right buttons'

The chances of success are significantly increased when the topic of the research fits closely with the specific priorities of the individual or organization evaluating the proposal. In the case of applications to funding organizations, there will be boundaries around the kind of research they support and, within these, they will probably have certain priority areas upon which they currently wish to focus their attention. Proposals that fall outside this area are not going to be successful. Similarly, where proposals are produced in connection with academic degrees, there are advantages to be gained by ensuring that the prospective supervisor can see a close link between the topic of the proposed piece of research and his or her own area of expertise. Potential supervisors are likely to prioritize proposals within their sphere of expertise because they are better able to evaluate the potential contribution and better able to supervise the research.

Whether the proposal is being written as part of an academic degree or as an application for research funding, the point to bear in mind is that what you personally believe to be worthwhile may not be the same as what is seen as worthwhile by the reader. In the context of writing a successful research proposal, however, it is the reader's view of what is interesting that is most important. The proposal, therefore, will stand a better chance of success where care is taken to *push the right buttons* and capture the attention of the reader. To accomplish this, it is useful to:

- check the supervisor's specialist area or the priority area of the funding body;
- know the current 'buzzwords' to include in the discussion;
- stick closely to any topic guidelines provided for the proposal.

Wider application

The value of a project will be enhanced when there is some clear link between the specific findings from the research and more general issues linked to the topic. The specific findings can be useful in their own right, perhaps addressing a practical problem or some localized concern. There is nothing wrong with this and, indeed, it can be a wise basis for proposals for bachelor's degree projects and master's degree dissertations. But, whatever the level of research for which the proposal is written, the value of the research will be enhanced when the proposal incorporates a vision of how the findings can be applied more generally.

The wider application of the findings will mean different things depending on the nature of the research that is being proposed. Broadly speaking, it can involve the quest to apply the particular findings (a) in a *practical* sense to other settings or (b) in a *theoretical* sense to the development of ideas and concepts linked to the topic. A wider practical application could involve a consideration of how far the findings from research in one location might be expected to apply in other similar locations, or perhaps different locations. Case studies of organizations will benefit where there is an explicit attempt to show how the findings might apply elsewhere in other organizations. A wider application in a theoretical sense could involve the use of the findings to develop or to criticize an existing theory on the topic. It could involve challenges to current beliefs or understandings about a topic, or it might even involve the generation of new ideas and concepts.

> **Top tip**
>
> The value of the research will be enhanced by the inclusion of statements in the proposal that demonstrate a conscious effort to apply the findings in a practical or theoretical way beyond the immediate context of the proposed research.

Precision

Research proposals need to be precise so that readers have the relevant information on which to judge whether the research will be worthwhile or feasible. Where readers need to evaluate the proposal, it is vital that they are provided with a crystal-clear vision of exactly what is being proposed because they need to have all the relevant facts at their disposal in order to decide whether or not the proposal is worthwhile: no-one would expect them to make decisions on the basis of guesswork. If the proposal offers only a vague impression of what is being proposed – fuzzy on detail or lacking in relevant facts and figures – they will be rightly suspicious about the value of the research and will have good reason to reject the proposal.

One aspect of this precision is reflected in the plan of work that is outlined in a research proposal. It is reasonable to suggest that a precise plan is going to be of far greater value than a loose plan. Precision, in this context, is the outcome of the kind of planning that is necessary for successful research. It means that the researcher has a clear vision of what is going to be studied and how it will be investigated. And it is exactly this point that will influence those who judge whether a proposal should be approved or not. They need to be convinced that the proposed research has been carefully thought through and that the researcher has a good grasp of what needs to be done and how it will be done. Information needs to be provided on the data that are to be collected (who, what, where, when, how many), and this information should be precise. Do not use words like 'try' or 'hope'. Use something more positive and definite like 'will' or 'intend'. And do not use words like 'some' and 'many' because they are vague. State a specific amount. Although it might not be possible to state exact details in advance, good proposals always provide *anticipated* numbers and amounts.

> **Top tip**
>
> Use words that are specific and positive.

A second aspect of precision concerns the ideas and concepts that are being used; there should be no room for ambiguity on this score. This means paying close attention to:

- *Definitions*: The research is almost certain to involve key terms and concepts and great care should be taken to define them precisely (see Chapter 5: Literature Review).
- *Research questions or hypotheses*: Good proposals manage to convert broad ideas about research into very precise statements about the specific things that will be focused upon to shed light on the research problem. Hypotheses or research questions serve this function (see Chapter 6: Research Questions).

A proposal that contains precise information, then, sends all the right *signals* to the readers. It provides them with what they need to know and what they expect to see. And, of course, the opposite is equally true: if a proposal lacks precision, the message this sends is that the proposal has been thrown together at the last moment by someone who cannot be bothered to pay attention to detail. So it is important for a proposal to *convey* a sense of precision and detail because this says to the reader that the proposal should be taken seriously.

Top tip
Improve the chances of success by providing precise information.

Summary of key points

Evaluators have two priorities in their minds when considering a research proposal: they want to know that the research will be worthwhile and they want to feel confident that the research is feasible. The task for the proposal is to reassure them on both points.

There are certain things that evaluators are likely to look for in a proposal as they ask themselves whether or not the research would be worthwhile. This chapter has outlined the importance in this respect of showing that:

- there is a *need* for the research;
- there are clear *benefits* to be gained from the research;
- *suitable methods* will be used to conduct the enquiry.

Evaluators will also look for information in the proposal that can help them decide whether the proposed research is feasible and, as we have noted, they will use their experience and expertise to weigh up the prospects for completion of the research bearing in mind the following:

- the scope and scale of the project;
- the available resources in terms of time and money;
- the ability to access data sources;
- the need for compliance with ethical, legal, and safety standards;
- the use of suitable planning and risk assessment procedures.

Success, however, might require something extra. Yes, success does depend on addressing a number of vital issues in the proposal to establish that the project is both worthwhile and feasible. But, in certain situations, this alone cannot guarantee that the proposal will be approved. If a proposal is submitted in a competitive environment where the evaluators need to be selective, its success will depend on it having something extra that makes it *distinctive* and that makes it 'stand out from the crowd'. This is the case particularly with funding bodies and PhD programmes where demand in terms of worthwhile and feasible proposals is likely to outstrip supply in terms of available money or places. Under such circumstances, the success of a proposal will depend on how far it can show that the research will have:

- elements of *originality* that make it different from what has already been done;
- *timeliness*, addressing current issues and being up-to-date;
- particular *relevance* for the evaluators, scratching where it itches and pushing the right buttons;
- *wider application*, linking the findings with more general practical or theoretical concerns;
- *precision*, avoiding any ambiguity or vagueness relating to definitions, data or planning.

Further reading

Fraenkel, J., Wallen, N. and Hyun, H. (2011) *How to Design and Evaluate Research in Education* (6th edn.). New York: McGraw-Hill (Chapter 24).

Leedy, P.D. and Ormrod, J.E. (2012) *Practical Research: Planning and Design International Edition* (10th edn.). Cambridge: Pearson (Chapters 1, 2).

Ogden, T.E. and Goldberg, I.A. (2002) *Research Proposals: A Guide to Success* (3rd edn.). San Diego, CA: Academic Press (Chapter 2).

3

SELLING AN IDEA

- *Advertising a product* • *Providing information* • *Target audience*
- *Value of good timing* • *Art of persuasion* • *Telling the truth*
- *Unique selling point* • *Sales pitch* • *Summary of key points*
- *Further reading*

As marketing experts tell us, it is not sufficient just to have a good product. That product needs to be *sold*. It needs to be brought to the attention of potential buyers and presented to them in a way that persuades them that this is a 'must have' item. In many senses, this applies to research proposals as much as it does to any other product. The product – in this case, the idea for research – might be good but the proposal will not be successful unless it can persuade the readers that what is on offer is something they want and need.

There is only a limited opportunity to do this persuasion. Because proposals are relatively brief, they have to quickly attract the interest of the reader and get the message across in a short time. In this respect, there is something of a 'sales pitch' built into good proposals. This is something to be borne in mind when writing a research proposal, and this chapter explores some of the lessons to be learned from marketing about how best to sell an idea for research.

Advertising a product

It is useful to think of a research proposal as an advertisement for a product. The product is the idea for a new piece of research, and this is to be advertised in the form of the proposal. Like an advertisement, the success of a proposal rests on its ability to *persuade* the audience to buy the product. In the case of a proposal, this does not necessarily mean to 'buy' the idea for a new piece of research in a literal sense. Funding proposals come pretty close to this because their success rests on their ability to persuade people to spend money on the idea. However, with other research proposals success involves 'buying' in a more metaphorical sense. It involves getting the audience to 'buy into' the idea – to accept it, agree with it, support it, and commit to it. The role of the research proposal, in either sense, is to act as a means of persuasion – convincing the audience that the thing on offer is *desirable* and something that they want to have.

Behind this point there is an assumption that readers might not automatically share an interest in, or enthusiasm for, the subject matter of the proposed research. They might be *open* to persuasion, but it should never be taken for granted that readers see things exactly the same as researchers do. Whatever the topic is, and however inherently interesting it might seem to be to the researcher, the task is to write the proposal in a way that *creates* an interest in the topic.

> **Top tip**
> Explain the context. Do not make unwarranted assumptions about what the reader knows or believes.

To continue the advertising analogy, success entails more than simply generating a wish for a product. It involves more than persuading the audience that the product is something they might want to have: they must be persuaded also that it is something that they *need*. The audience might not have realized that they needed the product before they saw the advertisement, but having seen the potential benefits of the product, they now understand that it is something they must have. A research proposal, in this sense, must entail *need recognition*.

Finally, the audience must be enticed to buy. They must go that extra step beyond recognizing the desirability of and need for a product – the extra step that involves action. They need to dig into their pockets and come up with the cash. Or, in the case of research proposals, they need to approve the proposal – often choosing it over other potential alternatives. The success of the proposal, then, involves persuading the audience into *action* in support of the research idea.

Providing information

Advertising's influence on the decision to buy a product is based on information about the nature of the product, its value, and its availability. In advertising, the factual aspect of the information can sometimes be subtle and oblique, with the advertisement cleverly getting over a message about the product in a way that might be entertaining and artistic and far from obvious. Other styles of advertising can hammer home a message in a much more explicit fashion using blunt facts about the product and its utility, about price and availability. There should be little doubt on this point that research proposals should accord more closely with the latter than the former approach to getting the message across. Research proposals should contain factual information and an explicit account of the research idea. Their audience should not be put in the position of trying to interpret the meaning of the message or of trying to infer what the benefits might be. Information needs to be laid out in a straightforward and unambiguous way. There is no benefit from trying to entertain the reader by holding back key bits of information until the end or making the reader *guess* how things will all fall into place. On the contrary, this will only frustrate readers who are trying to evaluate the proposal and invite them to conclude that the writer does not have a clear idea of what the research is trying to achieve or how it will try to achieve it.

> **Top tip**
> Be explicit about what will be done and why. Research proposals are not mystery novels.

People who evaluate research proposals tend to be under pressure – often being required to read many proposals one after another in a relatively short time. This is one factor that makes it necessary for research proposals to be relatively short documents. Normally, the maximum length of the proposal is stated quite explicitly by the organization involved. The Economic and Social Research Council (UK), for example, stipulates that 'On applications under £1 million, 6 sides of A4 for the case for support are allowed (12 sides of A4 for applications over £1 million).' By their nature, then, research proposals do not allow much space for researchers to make their case and get their message across. Every word needs to count and there is no room for waffle. Get to the point quickly.

> **Top tip**
> Keep things brief and precise.

In an effort to keep within strict word limits, there is the danger that researchers can start to pack their paragraphs full of references, concepts, and technical points in an attempt to impress the reader. If the style becomes too dense, though, there is a danger that the material can start to become hard to understand and even incomprehensible to the reader – who, remember, is likely to be working under pressures of time. This can frustrate and alienate the evaluator who, rather than being impressed by the proposal, is more likely to think that the researcher is unable to pick out the key issues and express them clearly. Clarity must not be sacrificed in the quest for brevity and precision. The trick is to get a balance between them. As Locke et al. (2000: 6) state: 'Simplicity, clarity, and parsimony are the standards of writing that reflect adequate thinking about the research problem. Complicated matters are best communicated when they are the objects of simple, well-edited prose.'

> **Top tip**
> Use straightforward language and focus on the key points.

Target audience

Advertisers talk of pitching their message to the right person, at the right time, and in the right place. They do so because they understand that their message can only be effective if it is addressed to an audience that is receptive and open to persuasion. What is worthwhile for one person might not be worthwhile for another and, as with advertisements, it is important to tailor the message to the particular needs of the key audience. The same applies with research proposals. The evaluators of the proposal need to be 'in tune' with the nature of the research and what it is trying to achieve, and the success of any proposal, it follows, will depend on there being a clear match between the content of the proposed research and the interests of those who will read it. If the proposal involves a funding bid, then clearly it has to be tailored to the specific areas of concern covered by the funding body to which it is sent. Applications to PhD programmes, equally, must go to faculties and professors whose areas of expertise match the subject area of the proposed research (see Table 3.1).

> **Top tip**
> Tailor the proposal to its specific audience.

Table 3.1 Targeting the research proposal: right time, right place

	Advertising	*Research proposal*
Item	product	idea for research
Target	right place right person	relevant funding body for the topic university/faculty interested in the topic supervisor with expertise on the topic
	right time	up-to-date topic addressing current concerns

Value of good timing

Hitting the right target is also a matter of *timeliness*. The agenda for research changes over time with certain issues and topics coming to prominence while others fade into the background. The likelihood of success of a proposal will be considerably improved if the chosen topic comes at a time when attention is being focused on that area. Funding bodies often highlight themes that they consider to be of particular significance for their current work, and these will change periodically. Applications for PhD programmes will obviously benefit when they are 'up-to-date' and deal with topics that are of current interest to university faculties and their professors (see Table 3.1).

Art of persuasion

At one level, it might appear very simple to meet the expectations of the audience. After all, the expectations are likely to be explicit and readily available in the form of guidelines for the completion of research proposals (which are produced by relevant organizations) or contained in the forms that need to be used for submitting a proposal. No need to second-guess what is required – it will be written down in black and white or available online. And, of course, it is very important to meet such requirements when writing a research proposal; they are hugely important in terms of the prospects of success.

> **Top tip**
> Check the formal requirements.

The art of persuasion, however, goes beyond the need to meet the formal requirements of the proposed research. Vital though this is, simply making sure that all the right boxes are ticked and that every requirement has been addressed may not be enough to guarantee success. A well-written research proposal will 'get inside the mind' of the readers of the proposal and envisage the things that they are likely to find attractive. Imagine yourself in the role of the evaluator of the proposal and then ask yourself if you would 'invest' in the proposed research.

- Will the necessary information be available for you to judge the quality of the proposed research?
- What would be the particular strengths of the proposal that might sell the idea to you?
- Are there any particular weaknesses that could deter you from buying into the research idea?

Top tip

Try to see things from the reader's point of view.

Convincing the audience about the value of the proposal also depends on writing skills and the researcher's ability to construct a *narrative* around the proposed work – to 'tell its story'. Literary skills are called in to play because selling the idea of the research is a lot easier if it is presented in a way that captures the interest of the reader and takes the reader on a journey of discovery, which leads them to understand the significance of the proposed research. The writing style and the sequencing of the argument can help to attract the attention of the reader. This is important because if the reader is bored or struggles to follow the logic of what is being written, he or she is likely to be turned off by the proposal.

Top tip

Create an interest in your research ideas.

Telling the story

Convey . . . your genuine interest, understanding and enthusiasm for the work. Keep the following questions in mind as you plan:

- what is the story that you are telling?
- what is the audience?
- why does it matter?
- why now?
- why you?

Advice from the UK Economic and Social Research Council on writing a research proposal.

Telling the truth

In terms of persuasion, there are two things that advertising might do that research proposals should never do. The first of these involves being explicit about what the product cannot do, as well as what it can do. Research proposals should never promise what they cannot deliver and should be open and explicit about their limitations. On this point, psychologists tell us that we are *more* likely to be persuaded if we feel we have been given the whole picture and alerted to both sides of the argument. So this will not damage the prospects of a research proposal being successful – only enhance it. The point to note, though, is that proposals are expected to state clearly what they will do, and also what they will *not* do.

Top tip
Acknowledge any limitations.

The second difference is that proposals need to be totally honest and transparent and should never involve statements designed to trick the reader into believing something that is not the case. The persuasion should never resort to *implying* things that are not true or cannot be substantiated, nor should it deliberately omit information that is known to have a bearing on the proposed research. Whereas advertising might make clever use of association and oblique references to conjure up a belief or feeling about a product, research proposals need to 'play it straight'.

Top tip
Honesty is essential.

Unique selling point

The unique selling point (also known as the 'unique selling proposition') is very important in terms of selling the product. The unique selling point is a feature of the product or service that allows it to stand out from others, that makes it special and gives it a unique identity. It is a distinctive feature of the product or service that gives it a competitive advantage in the market. It is something the competitors do not offer and it is a desirable thing that can be used through advertising to entice the audience to buy the product. Unique selling points can be linked to the nature of the product (specific uses, special functions, range of options), the services (fast delivery, personal attention) or the value (lowest price, lasts longer). Examples include Fairy washing-up liquid (lasts longer), Head and Shoulders™ shampoo (targets dandruff), and Maltesers® confectionery (light and non-fattening).

Research proposals, for their part, require a similar element of uniqueness to separate them from the others and give them some competitive advantage when it comes to gaining funding, getting selected or being approved. Being 'good enough' might be all right when there is no element of competition or scarce resources. But as soon as a research proposal is competing alongside others for limited money (funding proposals), limited places (PhD applications), restricted access (ethics approval) or the award of higher marks (projects and dissertations), the success of the proposal will owe something to its ability to establish in the mind of the audience that there is something unique about the research idea that makes it especially worthwhile and which makes it stand out from the crowd.

> **Top tip**
> Emphasize the difference and show that it matters.

Sales pitch

The art of persuading someone to buy into your idea, and to do so in a short space, has become popularized in the world of marketing as 'the elevator pitch'. When writing a research proposal, it provides a good analogy to keep in mind; the principles are very similar. The elevator pitch scenario is as follows. You step into a lift (elevator) in the lobby on the ground floor. In the lift is a senior business executive. You have the time it takes for the lift to travel from the lobby to the investor's offices on the top floor to make your pitch. You have just one or two minutes to persuade the business executive to invest in your product. To do this you have to:

- Explain precisely what you have to offer. (What is the 'need' that you can satisfy?)
- Be concise. (There is no time for waffle or anything but the key ideas.)
- Explain things clearly. (Avoid too much technical jargon; put things in a way that non-specialists can understand.)
- Promote the benefits. (In business terms, this will be couched in terms of sales potential, turnover and profits; in research, it will take the form of solving problems or contributions to knowledge.)
- Show enthusiasm and drive. (You must believe in what you are selling.)
- Answer the questions that will be foremost in the mind of potential investors. (Do not leave them with nagging doubts or a lack of information on crucial points.)

Examples of the sales pitch

The popular television series 'The Dragon's Den' (http://www.bbc.co.uk/ dragonsden) calls on budding businessmen and women to do a short sales pitch to persuade a panel of five wealthy entrepreneurs to invest in the product or service they have to offer. The time is short and, again, the task centres on persuading investors to buy into the particular (business) proposition. A web search for 'elevator pitch' provides similar examples of the sales pitch (e.g. http://www.youtube.com/watch?v=TqOtan49rmc).

Summary of key points

Good research proposals 'sell' an idea for research to their readers. They recognize the point that no matter how good the idea for research might be, the success of the proposal depends on its ability to communicate the idea in a fashion that will attract the attention of the readers and ultimately persuade them that the proposed research is a good idea. Successful proposals, in other words, need to work as an advertisement for the research, and we have seen in this chapter that there are a number of parallels between the art of advertising and the skill of writing a good research proposal. These are summarized in Table 3.2.

Table 3.2 Research proposals: an advertisement for a research idea

Advertising needs to:	Research proposals need to:
. . . be *brief*	. . . be *short*
. . . create *awareness*	. . . be *submitted* and hit the right target
. . . allow *comprehension*	. . . outline the *plan* for the research
. . . generate *interest*	. . . describe their *aims and objectives*
. . . foster a *desire*	. . . explain how they are *worthwhile and feasible*
. . . induce a *preference*	. . . show the *current need* for the research
. . . lead to *action* (product purchase)	. . . get *approval* and support

There are also some similarities, as the chapter has shown, between research proposals and a 'sales pitch'. Because both are quite short, they need to:

- grab the attention of the audience;
- convince them you have something worthwhile to 'sell';
- get the message over succinctly and clearly.

To achieve this, a research proposal – just like an advertisement or a sales pitch – needs to do three things. First, it needs to recognize the significance of the audience and the value of tailoring the message to suit the particular people who matter. It should be borne in mind that the success of any research proposal will depend on its ability to *communicate* with a specific *target audience* and to *persuade* them that the proposed research is something they need.

Second, the proposal needs to be written bearing in mind the evaluators' point of view. The researcher will benefit from trying to get some insight into what the evaluators will be looking for.

And third, the proposal needs to get the message across clearly. Readers should not have to flick back and forth through the proposal to piece together the information they need. It should be there, laid out on a plate in front of them. The proposal needs to tell them what they want to know, when they want to know it. Echoing again a similarity with advertising, good ideas need to be packaged and presented in a way that is well received by the audience and in essence this means:

- succinct expression, getting to the point quickly; and
- using a clear narrative that tells an interesting story.

Finally, there are some crucial limits to the analogy with advertising that must be taken into consideration. These are very important. Unlike advertising, research proposals should always:

- be totally honest;
- acknowledge limitations;
- require no guesswork on the part of the readers.

Further reading

Aronson, E. (1999) *The Social Animal*. New York: Worth (Chapter 3).
Cialdini, R. (2007) *Influence: The Psychology of Persuasion*. New York: Collins (Chapter 1).
Hatton, A. (2007) *The Definitive Business Pitch*. Harlow: Pearson (Chapters 1 and 8).
Kuhnke, E. (2012) *Persuasion and Influence*. Chichester: Wiley (Chapter 1).

II

HOW DO I PRODUCE A GOOD RESEARCH PROPOSAL?

4

AIMS OF THE RESEARCH

What is it all about?

• *Title* • *Keywords* • *Aims* • *Background* • *Summary of key points*
• *Further reading*

What is the research trying to do? This is the first thing that any readers of a proposal will wish to know. They will want to have this information in order to assess how worthwhile and how feasible the proposal is likely to be. Without knowing the aims of the research, they cannot possibly judge whether the methodology is appropriate or whether there will be sufficient time and resources to complete the project. So the research proposal needs to provide readers with the relevant information 'up front' near the beginning. Reflecting this need, information about the aims of the research is to be found in *the title* of the proposed project, in the *keywords* associated with the investigation, in the statement of *aims*, and in the description of the *background* to the research.

Title

The title is the headline-selling feature of any proposal and its importance is hard to overstate. It is the most prominent and most immediate statement about the proposed research that the reader will see – and first impressions count. Within the space of a few words the researcher has to capture the essence of the research 'in a nutshell' and it is vital, therefore, that the title should be clear, accurate, and precise.

Clarity

A crucial quality of a good title is that it should be straightforward and presented in a way that can be easily understood. When it comes to research proposals, there should be no chance of misinterpretation, no element of ambiguity. The meaning should be crystal-clear.

In practice, there are certain things that it is worth bearing in mind in this respect. First and foremost, the words that are chosen for the title should be correct in terms of language. Because it is a headline for the research, it is vital that the title contains *no errors of grammar or spelling*. Any such error in the title will send a damaging message to readers about the quality of the research proposal that is to follow. The second thing is that titles normally avoid the use of *acronyms*. Although there are some circumstances where this is permissible, the general advice is to avoid them because their use does open up the possibility of misunderstanding. For example, the use of 'IT' in a title could refer to 'Information Technologies' or to 'Intermediate Treatment'. Although the exact meaning will become apparent subsequently in the proposal, in the title itself it is generally safer to spell out the term in full to avoid any possibility of confusion. A third thing to consider is that titles should not try to be entertaining or clever if this compromises the clarity of the title. Bear in mind that proposals are serious, formal documents used in relation to academic awards, funding applications, and ethical approval. This is not really the context to use humorous language, puns or other kinds of clever eye-catching headlines that might be better suited to newspapers and magazines. Even titles that take the form of a question are frowned upon by many readers. There is no absolute rule that says such things are totally unacceptable but the point to appreciate is that a sense of gravitas can pay dividends in terms or sending the right message to those who will evaluate the proposal. It says, 'This proposal is serious – treat it seriously.'

> **Top tip**
> Keep things serious and straightforward.

Accuracy

Titles should accurately portray the proposed research. Although this might seem glaringly obvious, there are often occasions when the nature of what is being proposed in the body of the proposal does not quite match with what has been stated in the title. This is a serious problem because the readers will have their vision of the project shaped by the title and will then be surprised and frustrated if what is actually presented in the body of the proposal does not faithfully reflect that title. They might think that the researcher is trying to fool them about the real nature of the research – although this is pretty unlikely. More probably, the readers will infer that the researcher does not really have a clear vision of the project and that the mismatch is a result of some muddled thinking about what the research is really all about. In either case, any mismatch will send a bad signal to those who evaluate the proposal and will definitely harm the proposal's prospects of success.

> **Top tip**
> Check that the title matches the content. Ideas develop and change during the course of planning a project. So when you have finished writing the proposal go back to the beginning, look at the title afresh and make sure that it still accurately depicts the research you propose to do.

Precision

There is a delicate balancing act to be performed when constructing a title for a project. On the one hand, there is a need to keep things brief, while on the other, there is a need to provide sufficient detail. If the title is too brief, it will not satisfy the need for precision because inevitably it will be wide in terms of its scope and not contain enough information about the specific nature of the inquiry. If it is too long, it will probably deter people from reading on and worry those who evaluate the proposal about the researcher's ability to capture the essence of the project 'in a nutshell'. This, after all, is what the title is required to do.

To accomplish this balancing act, the titles for research proposals tend to adopt a particular format. Again, there is no absolute rule that dictates they must always do so, but there is a convention about the construction of titles that it would be prudent to observe. This involves dividing the title into two components, which are separated by a colon (:). These components consist of:

- a *main title* outlining the general area of the research;
- a supplement that includes more specific information. This tends to be a bit longer and to include more specific details about things such as the factors being investigated, the methods being used, the location, and the time scale of the study.

Overall, titles tend to be around ten to thirty words in length, and the following examples indicate what conventional titles might look like:

Motivation in the workplace: A case study of full-time and part-time employees in a department store in Aberdeen

Household income and educational attainment: A comparison of examination success rates for A-level students in five cities in England and Wales, 2012

Uncertain identities and health-risking behaviour: A survey of young people and smoking in the era of late modernity

Keywords

In the context of a research proposal, 'keywords' are things that denote the content of the proposed research in a way that can be used when searching indexes, directories, and catalogues. They usually consist of three to six terms that pinpoint the core ideas behind the research. They are presented either as a list of bullet points, or as a series of words on a single line. Although it is not their primary function, keywords can be useful for those who evaluate proposals because they provide a brief but carefully considered insight into the core features of the proposed research. Like the title, keywords also capture the essence of the research 'in a nutshell'.

Keywords do not have to be individual words; it is quite common to find that a keyword can consist of two or three words, which, when combined, specify a concept or issue that can be recognized for the purposes of defining what the research is about. So a keyword might be something like 'supply-chain management', 'health-related behaviour' or 'educational achievement'. If we were to separate these words, they would not work. The individual components would not help to provide useful search results. Combined, however, they serve as valuable 'keywords' that could be used for indexing purposes.

A useful way of envisaging what the keywords might be is to imagine that the proposed research has already been conducted and that it is available online on the web. Now, if someone wanted to locate this work using an Internet search engine, which terms would they need to enter to bring up a link to the research at the top of the list? These are the terms that can be used as keywords.

> **Top tip**
> Think of the keywords as terms you would use to search online for your research.

One further point is worth mentioning with regard to keywords. In practice, they are likely to echo some of the words in the title. This is not a problem. Indeed, it would be troubling if the keywords did not appear also in the title because this might suggest that the title is not doing its job of describing exactly what the research is all about. So, some overlap between the words in the title and the keywords is a good thing. For example, if the title of the proposed research was

> The perceived risks of online banking: A survey of online shopping behaviour and bank customers' feelings about security and fraud in relation to their use of Internet banking

the keywords might include:

> online shopping, Internet banking, shopping behaviour, customer satisfaction, banking security, Internet fraud

Aims

The aims (or 'purpose statement') of the research indicate the direction in which the research will go and point to the target that the research hopes to hit. In doing this, they guide the reader's expectations about the nature of the proposed investigation. There is no need at this point to justify the choice of topic or explain why the research will be conducted in a specific manner. That can be done in the Background section (where the substantive, practical issues can be described) and the Literature Review (where the existing theories and evidence can be used to justify the approach adopted by the proposed research). At this stage, the idea is simply to provide the bare outlines of where the research is hoping to go.

Types of research aims

It is important to be clear about which type of aim is being pursued by the proposed research. From the reader's point of view, this helps to provide a clear picture of the overall purpose of the research. It is also important because different types of aims call for different approaches to the research; they tend to be associated with different research traditions or paradigms. Within any statement about the aims of research, therefore, it is good practice to identify clearly whether the research is attempting to do one or more of the following:

- explain the causes or consequences of something;
- criticize or evaluate some theory or belief;
- describe something;
- forecast some outcome;
- develop good practice;
- empower a social group.

Scope and scale of research aims

The list of aims not only shows the direction in which the research will go, it also provides an indication of the scale and scope of the proposed investigation. In doing so, it should alert the readers to the size of the task the researcher is planning to embark upon. There is a danger here that, in an effort to do research that is perceived as worthwhile, the researcher might get too ambitious. It is a common mistake to set targets that cannot reasonably be achieved within the available time and resources. It is important, therefore, to ensure that the aims that are stated have been scoped and that they are realistically achievable.

Link up with **Delimitations and scoping the research**, p. 69

Link up with **The scale of the project**, p. 111

Presentation of aims

The research aims can be written as a paragraph using normal prose. Although there is nothing wrong with this, another style of presenting research aims uses a list of phrases, each of which starts with a verb – a verb that is particularly relevant for research activity. This has become conventional and is more likely to meet the expectations of those who evaluate proposals. There are normally about three to six of these phrases.

Whether using normal prose or using a list of bullet points, it is better to start the list with the broadest of the aims, and then put the list in a logical sequence. So, in the example below, the list starts with the broad aim of conducting research into mass transport systems. This establishes at the start what the whole thing is about. Even at this stage, though, this is qualified by restricting the area of interest to large cities. Next on the list we see that this particular research will focus on one aspect of mass transport systems – buses. And, specifically, it will look at the phenomenon of bunching on urban routes. How will this be done? Well, the subsequent bullet points indicate the approach that will be taken towards achieving the aims.

Example: Research into mass transport systems

- *To investigate* the effectiveness of mass transport systems in large cities.
- *To study*, in particular, the bunching of buses on urban routes.
- *To describe* the frequency and impact of bunching on urban routes.
- *To analyse* the causes of bunching using probability statistics and queueing theory.
- *To understand* the responses to bunching by bus drivers.
- *To develop* recommendations for reducing the incidence of bunching on urban routes.

General

Specific

Background

To understand what the research 'is all about', readers need to know something about the background (or the 'problem statement') to the research. On many occasions, of course, they will be aware of the situation already. But proposals should never take for granted what readers already know. They should operate, instead, on the premise that some readers might *not* know the circumstances surrounding the proposed research and that it is not clear to them why a specific piece of research is being proposed. To avoid this prospect, good research proposals always ensure that the background to the research is stated explicitly and clearly so that *all* readers of the proposal should be able to understand the rationale for the research.

> **Top tip**
> Do not make too many assumptions about what the reader might know about the subject area of the research.

Context

The Background section provides an opportunity to outline the context within which the research will take place. Depending on the nature of the proposed research, this can focus on the historical background and look at developments that have preceded the project. Alternatively, it can focus on contemporary circumstances within which the research is to take place. And on many occasions the Background section will incorporate elements of both the historical and the contemporary context. What matters most is that it blends together the kind of background information that most usefully explains to the readers *the bigger picture*. This can involve locating the proposed research within one or more of the following contexts:

- *Historical context*: Are there particular events or trends that provide a backdrop to the research (e.g. a banking crisis, an ecological threat, an environmental disaster)?
- *Policy context*: Do recent changes in policies, regulations, laws or political views need to be recognized to understand the purpose of the research?
- *Practical problems*: Does the research arise in response to certain practical problems, such as within a work setting, or does it look for new ways of doing things that address such problems?
- *Key ideas*: Are there particular theories, authors or opinion leaders whose ideas form a backdrop to the proposed research?

It is worth emphasizing that the Background section might well include a combination of more than one of these kinds of contextual information.

> **Top tip**
> Use the Background section to set the scene for the proposed research.

Evidence, events, and publications

The account of the context should not only be clear and concise, it should also include some *evidence*. It is good practice to support the argument being made by:

- citing publications linked with prominent theories/writers/approaches in the field;
- noting the findings from recent published research in the area;
- using relevant data, including facts and figures (for example, to do with trends, prevalence rates, proportions, volumes);
- referring to key events;
- specifying details of relevant legislation, regulations, policies, and official reports.

By incorporating reference to such things within the Background section, the researcher provides supporting *evidence* relating to the context of the proposed research. The persuasiveness of the case being presented by the researcher does not depend on the reader simply accepting the researcher's impression of how significant and beneficial the proposed research might be. The case is now bolstered by drawing on key published works, backed up by hard facts and figures, and directly linked to events in the real world.

How many references and how much data should be included? Obviously, given the constraints of space, there should be no attempt to develop a discussion drawing together the major themes and research findings associated with the topic – that is something more suited to a literature review (see Chapter 5). But a few well-chosen bits of supporting evidence can have a significant impact on the credibility afforded to the research and on the prospects of the proposal being successful.

Top tip

Provide some evidence to support your account of the background to the research.

Selecting the most significant points

Clearly, it is not possible to cover every aspect of the context because this would take too long and, more significantly, it would not really help to explain to the reader why the particular piece of research being proposed is significant. In practice, the researcher needs to be *selective* about what to include and what not to include. Being selective means making choices and judgements about which of the many contextual factors are the most relevant. This can be a demanding task. Inevitably, within the constraints of the space available, it requires the researcher to include only the most important points. The consequence of this is that the researcher needs to make brave decisions about what to leave out. There is not the space to 'play safe' and include lots of material just in case it ought to be there. When writing the Background section, the researcher needs to decide what are the most important things for selling the idea of the research and which things are less crucial.

Summary of key points

The aims of the research are specified near the beginning of the proposal. They are covered in the:

- Title
- Keywords
- Statement of aims
- Background.

Those who evaluate research proposals will expect to find the aims presented in a clear and succinct manner, readily available and easy to find. This is because the aims are the starting point from which readers can proceed to (a) understand what the research is all about, and (b) make subsequent judgements about the quality of the proposed research questions and research methods.

There are certain conventions surrounding the ways that the Title, the Keywords, the Statement of aims, and the Background section are presented, and the chances of success for the proposal will be increased when these conventions are recognized and followed.

The title is the first thing that readers encounter in relation to a research proposal and it is vital, therefore, that it conveys the right information about the research. It is worth spending time making sure that the title has three qualities. It should be: (a) clear, (b) accurate, and (c) precise.

The keywords should be three to six words, or combinations of words, that most accurately depict the content of the overall research. Although they are primarily concerned with matters of indexing and bibliographic searches, the keywords can also help readers to pinpoint exactly what the research is all about. In either case, it is in the researcher's interest to make sure that the keywords are appropriate.

In terms of the Aims, it is conventional to present them as a series of 'one-line' phrases starting with verbs such as 'To contribute to . . .', 'To describe . . .', 'To analyse . . .'. The sequencing of the aims normally sees the overarching aims presented first with subsequent aims getting progressively more narrow and specific in terms of their goals. This manner of spelling out the aims is not a hard and fast rule; researchers can describe the aims in other ways as well.

But it is a manner with which most evaluators will feel both familiar and comfortable, and sticking to the convention is more likely than not to meet the expectations of the readers.

Turning attention from *how* the aims are expressed to *what* they express, we noted earlier in the chapter that there are certain 'types' of aims that correspond with styles of research. It may not be possible, or desirable, to pigeon-hole all projects by pinning them down to being one type or another, but it is helpful for the purposes of clarity if the proposal is aligned with one or more of the well-established types of research,

The importance of avoiding over-ambitious aims has been stressed in this chapter. It is important not to get carried away and suggest that the project will cover a massive range of issues. The scope and scale of the proposed research should be narrow enough to render the research feasible – tailored to suit the available time and money for conducting the investigation.

Finally, the Background section sets the scene for the research. It describes the context within which the research will take place and helps to make the case that the research will be worthwhile. Principally it should:

- describe the circumstances within which the proposed research has emerged;
- introduce some evidence supporting the case that there is a need for the proposed research;
- argue that the proposed research meets that need and is thus worthwhile.

Further reading

Creswell, J.W. (2009) *Research Design: Qualitative, Quantitative, and Mixed Methods Approaches* (3rd edn.). Thousand Oaks, CA: Sage (Chapter 5).

Lyons Morris, L. and Taylor Fitz-Gibbon, C. (1978) *How to Deal with Goals and Objectives*. Beverly Hills, CA: Sage (Chapters 1–3).

Marshall, C. and Rossman, G. (2006) *Designing Qualitative Research* (4th edn.). Thousand Oaks, CA: Sage (Chapter 2).

5

LITERATURE REVIEW

What do we already know?

• *What literature should be included?* • *Literature search* • *What if nothing has been written on the topic?* • *How do I 'review' the publications?* • *An iterative process* • *What message should the literature review contain?* • *Delimitations and scoping the research* • *Summary of key points* • *Further reading*

The literature review examines key ideas, key issues, and key findings contained in publications relevant to a specific area of study. The purpose is to find out what we already know about the subject matter of the proposal and to use this as the basis for deciding the specific things that the research can look at to make a worthwhile contribution to the topic.

Within the confines of a research proposal any literature review will be preliminary: it will provide a basic starting point that lays the foundation for the proposed research. This is the inevitable consequence of two things. First, research proposals are relatively brief documents and there are normally quite tight constraints on the number of words/pages that the researcher is allowed to devote to the review. This means that the discussion must focus on just the most central and significant pieces of published work.

Second, the proposal is a plan for research and it is written before the investigation gets under way. There is a practical limit to how much time and effort can be put into the literature review in preparation for the research compared with how much effort will be put into it once the proposal has been approved and the project has begun. In the case of bachelor's research projects and master's dissertations, the bulk of the review tends to take place after the proposal has been accepted – during the time allocated to the research project or dissertation itself. When proposals are written for entry to a PhD programme or as part of a funding bid then they will be expected to be longer, cover a wider number of sources, and be more developed. Even here, though, work on the literature review will occur after the application has been accepted and it will continue during the lifetime of the project.

It is thus important to recognize that, in terms of both length and timing, there is a distinction to be made between the literature review as it appears in a research proposal – which provides a brief, preliminary review – and the more developed literature review that will appear in any final report that is written at the end of the project.

> For research proposals, the literature review tends to be preliminary. In most cases, it will be continued and extended as part of the project once the project has gained approval and got underway.

What literature should be included?

How much?

There is no fixed rule about how many works should be included in a literature review. But to provide some 'ballpark' figure for guidance a proposal is likely to include reference to somewhere between five and 20 sources. The number might vary depending on the particular subject area of the proposal and it is also worth bearing in mind that the number will be considerably lower than that which will eventually appear in the full literature review produced at the end of the project. The numbers here could be around 50 for an undergraduate project, 100 for a master's dissertation, and 250 for a PhD thesis. At the proposal stage, though, the aim is basically to provide a *prima facie* case that the proposed research is worthwhile and feasible.

Top tip

Check how many sources are generally included in similar proposals. Prospective supervisors should be able to offer advice in this respect, or there might be some guidance given on the proposal form itself.

Which ones?

Selecting which works to include and which to exclude is an important strategic decision as far as the proposal is concerned. The fact is that relatively few sources can be included, and the ones that are chosen need to do three things. First, they need to convey to the reader the purpose of the research and its potential value. Second, they need to persuade the reader that the researcher has acquired a reasonable knowledge about the proposed area of research and that the proposal builds upon relevant findings from past research and addresses themes that are attracting attention at the moment. Third, they need to present the right kind of profile of sources that readers will recognize as a suitable foundation for the proposed research. Pulling this off can be challenging, but there are some broad questions about the sources that can help to guide the overall selection of works. For example:

- Do the selected sources include some core, well-established works that act as signposts to the direction of the research and demonstrate the researcher's familiarity with the subject area?
- Are there some recent works that show familiarity with current developments in the field and indicate that the proposed research is up-to-date?
- Is there a balance of books, articles, and online sources that are appropriate for the field of investigation?

What types?

For the purposes of projects, dissertations, and theses, the works that are referred to should be those that come from *published sources that are authoritative and credible.* This means that the researcher should be looking for sources of material that come from:

- books (monographs, edited volumes, textbooks);
- academic journals (refereed articles);
- conference proceedings (especially in fast-moving subject areas such as computing and information technologies);
- academic theses and dissertations;
- practitioner journals (those of professional bodies, e.g. medicine, law);
- official publications (government publications, United Nations and European Union publications, policy documents, law reports);
- reference materials (subject dictionaries, encyclopaedias).

Publication, in its own right, can no longer be treated as a criterion that makes something worthy of inclusion in a literature review. In the past, a publication generally involved the idea of a printed article or book that was professionally produced by a publishing company. The Internet, however, has opened up an avenue for making literature publicly available without the involvement of a publishing company and, today, practically anyone can publish something on the web. As a consequence, it is now the *credibility of the source* of the publication that is crucial and the researcher needs to be discriminating when it comes to the type of publication that is considered worthy of including in the literature review.

Official publications from government departments tend to be regarded as fairly safe and reliable sources to include in a literature review. Articles in academic journals, likewise, will be considered appropriate. This is because they normally go through a review process involving experts in the field – they are 'refereed' to check their quality. Works that have been published in traditional formats (books) by publishing companies that have established reputations are also considered credible. The publishing process generally involves quality checks that mean the researcher can, within bounds, treat such sources as credible. When it comes to material available online through the Internet, however, the researcher needs to be particularly careful to evaluate the source. In the context of a literature review, it is likely that government websites and the websites of major international non-governmental organizations (such as the United Nations) will tend to have more credibility than, for instance, Wikis or websites created by an individual.

Literature search

There are five ways of identifying the main published material on a specific topic:

Expert advice. As a good starting point, there is no simpler or more effective way of finding out which authors and which theories are the most important than to seek expert advice. Students can seek advice from their *supervisors* and can refer to lecture notes provided by tutors as a straightforward departure point for their initial search.

Internet searches. The simplicity of conducting searches using the Internet makes it an attractive option for researchers. Using suitable *keywords* (see Chapter 4), it can be highly productive, opening up access to relevant literature on a global scale and including the latest research from a huge variety of sources. For academic articles, Google Scholar is useful. For information on concepts and ideas, Wikipedia offers a starting point. For general information, any of the search engines can be employed. And for details of published books, the websites of online book retailers can be trawled (e.g. Amazon, eBay, the Book Depository).

References in textbooks. Textbooks identify crucial works on particular topics and they frequently contain suggestions for further reading at the end of each chapter. In these ways, they steer the researcher towards works that are regarded as particularly important and relevant within the area of study.

Online databases. Online databases include bibliographies, indexes, and archives that contain compiled lists of books, articles, abstracts, and many kinds of documents of value to researchers. They usually have advanced search facilities based on topics, authors, dates, and type of publication. The researcher ought to check early on whether a bibliography already exists that covers the topic to be investigated. Libraries are the obvious place to check first. Access to databases can be restricted but researchers linked to universities can obtain wide-ranging access to online databases.

Review articles. Review articles map out the area by identifying the main issues, the core themes, the key authors, and the key studies associated with a particular topic. They provide expert opinion and a 'state of the art' commentary on current ideas that relative newcomers can use as a foundation for their own inquiries. Another reason to use existing review articles is that they can be used as examples of how to do a review. They will illustrate how to analyse, synthesize, and draw conclusions from the literature.

Top tip

Look for existing review articles on the topic.

A systematic approach to the search

It is good practice to approach the search for literature in a systematic fashion and to explain how the literature will be found. The account does not need to be very detailed. It only needs to identify the databases used and the keywords used for searches. But this is important because it serves to reassure those who evaluate the research proposal that the research will not have been guided by some haphazard approach that could all too easily have missed key sources of information.

> **Top tip**
>
> Describe the search process you have used. It needs to be 'transparent' and open to scrutiny by the readers.

What if nothing has been written on the topic?

It is virtually impossible to find a topic on which nothing of relevance has been written. Bearing this in mind, it would be disastrous in the context of a research proposal to say that 'nothing has been written on this topic'. This is not to deny the fact that if the topic is quite narrowly defined or based on a specific instance (e.g. a company, a city), then a literature search might produce a nil return. Indeed, in one respect this is actually a good thing because it would mean that there is some new contribution to be made by the research. It is not replicating work that has been done already. But this should never lead the researcher to conclude that there are no publications to include in the review. Research proposals operate on the premise that there will always be published works that are *related* to the topic or which have a bearing on how the topic can be investigated. So, for example, if a literature search for research into 'customer satisfaction among customers of the Costalot energy supply company' were to reveal no previous publications on this exact topic, this should not be taken to mean that 'nothing has been published on the topic'. Instead, as Table 5.1 shows, the search should proceed to look for literature that is of *relevance* for different *aspects* of the topic.

> **Top tip**
>
> If you think there is nothing written on your chosen topic, think again!

Table 5.1 Literature of relevance to a research topic: an example
'Customer satisfaction among customers of the Costalot energy supply company'

Search procedure	Literature sources of relevance to the topic			
Search on sub-component #1 'Customer satisfaction'	Publications dealing with the significance of customer satisfaction and/or how to conduct research into it	Examples of customer satisfaction surveys conducted elsewhere	Business theories underlying a belief in the benefits of customer satisfaction
Search on sub-component #2 'Costalot'	Information relating to use of Costalot as a case study: is it typical of energy supply companies?	Information about the company	Information about competitors
Search on sub-component #3 'Energy supply company'	Publications on the broad business environment in which energy supply companies currently operate	Economic and technical issues currently facing energy supply companies in general	Policy documents relating to political pressure encouraging competition between energy supply companies

How do I 'review' the publications?

Analyse the material

Having searched for sources that appear to be relevant to the topic of the research, the researcher is then faced with the task of reviewing this literature. This task should be undertaken in a systematic fashion. It needs to be systematic in the sense that, from the start, attention needs to be paid to logging the bibliographic details of publications and collecting vital details about the aims, methods, and findings of the works. The researcher needs to have a system for collecting and cataloguing the various works that he or she reads and which might be eligible for inclusion in the review. There are a variety of computer software programs that have come to be essential tools for research in terms of their capacity for storing, searching, and retrieving such information. Word-processing packages, spreadsheets, and databases can all be used inventively to manage literature, but packages are available that have a dedicated functionality for searching and managing research literature (e.g. End-Note, Mendeley, Zotero).

> **Top tip**
> Use a suitable software package to manage your research literature.

A thorough and systematic approach to storing, searching, and retrieving the research literature provides a good foundation for the review. But the success of a review really owes more to the creative intellectual skill of analysing and evaluating the works. It is not sufficient to simply describe what various authors have written and leave it at that. Certainly, it is important as part of any research project to have a summary of the ideas and research findings linked with key writers who have contributed to what is currently known about a particular topic. But within the literature review the aim is to go beyond this. Rather than providing a list of who said what, the idea is to *analyse* the material. The process of analysis involves searching for the component parts that make up the whole entity that is being studied, and in practice this means that the review should be looking for *themes* running through the works that are being reviewed. So, rather than describing the content of each work that is being included in the review, the aim should be to map out the area and take an overview of the works and ask what they represent as a whole:

Mapping out the area:

- What are the key studies and who are the main authors in the area?
- What are the key theories and perspectives running through the literature?
- What are the core issues and problems addressed by the literature?

Taking an overview of the area:

- What are the common areas of agreement among the authors?
- What are the overall findings from their research?
- Where are the areas of disagreement, contradictions, and gaps in the material?
- What new research might be valuable to move things forward?

Top tip

Don't just list what others have said and done. The literature review is not a catalogue or inventory of items. The idea is to compare and contrast the works, to look for common elements, and to note what strengths and weaknesses there are in the works.

Be critical

A review of the literature requires the researcher to adopt a critical stance. Being critical does not necessarily mean that the researcher should focus on the shortcomings of particular authors or deride their work. As Wallace and Wray

(2011) suggest, it is more to do with approaching the existing material in an open-minded fashion – neither convinced of its truth nor determined to prove it wrong. Claims are not accepted at face value but are accepted depending on the ability of the author to present evidence and mobilize a good argument that supports their position. Before being persuaded that an author's ideas or findings are valid, the reviewer needs satisfactory answers to questions such as:

• Are the authors' claims warranted? Are they backed up by sufficient evidence and reasoning?
• Is enough information given about the methods used to collect and analyse their data?
• Are the authors impartial and objective? How far do their values shape their conclusions?
• How recent is the work and how relevant are its findings for today's circumstances?
• How far is it reasonable to generalize from the particular findings?

Top tip

Criticize the ideas, not the authors. Don't get personal. It's the ideas that matter.

Draw conclusions

Conclusions, by definition, occur at the end of things and so it is with conclusions within a literature review – they are the last part of the review. But the idea of a conclusion also involves a *judgement or deduction* arrived at on the basis of some preceding deliberation and it is this that lies at the heart of the matter. Good reviews draw conclusions. They do not leave strands of the discussion 'hanging in mid-air', nor do they 'sit on the fence'. They bring things to an end by reaching some judgement or deduction based on the analysis of the literature that has been undertaken.

In the context of research proposals such conclusions should normally point to a number of research questions. The review of the literature, properly done, will lead to the conclusion that there are certain questions that need to be answered or issues that need to be addressed. And, of course, these are precisely the questions and issues that are being promoted as worthy of investigation by the research proposal.

Link up with **Chapter 6: Research Questions**

An iterative process

As it appears in a research proposal, a literature review contains a narrative – a story that unfolds in a logical sequence to persuade the reader that the proposed research is worthwhile. The persuasiveness of the review depends a great deal on making a solid case for the proposed research that is neat and contains no 'loose ends'. But this is the end-product. It shrouds a messy reality in which a literature review normally goes through a series of re-writes, a process of refining the argument, a development that sees new material introduced and some edited out. In practice, writing a literature review tends to be something of an *iterative* process involving a cycle of repetition in which the researcher frequently revisits the literature and revises the research questions, as Figure 5.1 indicates.

FIGURE 5.1 The Literature Review: an iterative process

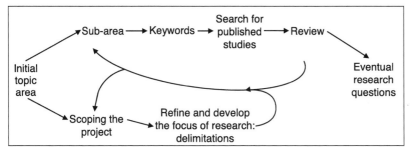

What message should the literature review contain?

Despite its preliminary nature, the literature review plays a vital role in any research proposal. It may be shorter and it may be less developed than the full review but it serves similar functions concerned with establishing that the research is *worthwhile*. In the process of 'selling an idea' the proposal needs to persuade the reader that the topic of the investigation is something that matters and that the research is likely to produce some outcome that has clear and specific benefits. Proposals need to pre-empt questions about the value of conducting the research and address sceptical concerns that readers might have about what is to be gained, who benefits, what is the value-added, and why bother – and this is where the literature review plays a vital role. It helps to sell the idea of the research.

Show that there is a need for the proposed research

The aim of the literature review within a research proposal is to develop an argument that there is a *need* for the proposed research. This means that the reader should be able to see a case for the research that is reasonable 'at first sight' – something that deserves to be considered.

There are broadly four ways in which this can be done. These are not mutually exclusive, but they do provide distinct ways of reviewing the available literature to provide a rationale for the proposed research. It can be argued that the proposed research:

- *Builds upon existing knowledge* – using the findings from previous research as a platform for expanding our knowledge base. Existing research work provides the foundation upon which to increase our stock of knowledge and the aim of the literature review is to show how the proposed research will extend what we know already.
- *Fills a gap in existing knowledge* – using the findings from previous re-search to identify areas that have been overlooked so far. At first glance, this might seem similar to the aim of building upon existing knowledge but the emphasis is more on finding new areas for research rather than staying on the path mapped out by existing research findings in a field.
- *Adopts a critical stance* – reviewing the existing material with the aim of revealing the shortcomings and inadequacies of existing knowledge. The flaws within existing research might well owe something to the areas they do not cover and, in this respect, the critical stance has the aim of filling a gap in existing knowledge. However, the critical stance goes further, pointing to the flaws in earlier investigations and suggesting that an alternative approach has the potential to provide a different and better way of understanding the particular topic.
- *Tackles a problem* – applying the knowledge from existing research to a practical problem for which a remedy is important. In the process of using what is already known as a means for dealing with a problem, there is potential to develop new knowledge in the form of recommendations and guidelines emerging from the research.

Argue that the proposed research meets that need

There is a distinction to be drawn between showing that there is a need for a particular piece of research and persuading the reader that what is contained in the research proposal meets that need. That is why it is vitally important that when reviewing the literature the proposed research is presented as 'fit for purpose' – linking what needs to be done to what is proposed should be done. Three things need to be borne in mind in this respect. The review should:

- show how the research is *timely* – arguing that the subject matter of the proposed research is of particular significance in relation to contemporary events;
- establish that the proposed methods are *suitable* – pointing towards the contribution that can be made by the kind of research that is being proposed;
- arrive at a *conclusion* – drawing together the threads of the discussion to arrive at a logical conclusion that points to the need for particular research questions to be investigated in order to 'fill in the gaps', 'take things further' or 'do a better job than has been done so far'. It is all too easy to assume the points have been made rather than capitalize on them by drawing things together with a powerful concluding statement.

> **Top tip**
> Use the literature review to argue that the research is needed and worthwhile doing.

Demonstrate your familiarity with key ideas in the area of study

Readers of a proposal will wish to feel assured that the researcher knows what he or she is talking about and is competent to embark on the proposed research. The review of literature has a role to play here. Properly done, the review demonstrates a familiarity with the main issues and debates in the field, and this can bolster the reader's confidence about the likely success of the proposed research. The degree of familiarity, of course, can be expected to vary depending on whether the proposal is written for a bachelor's project, a master's dissertation, a PhD application or a research funding bid but, in all cases, the literature review gives an indication of what the researcher knows about the topic on which he or she proposes to conduct research.

Identify the intellectual origins of the work

The literature review serves to 'map out' the area of the proposed research and the approach that is to be taken to the investigation. It pinpoints the theories, ideas, and practices that shape the proposed research and, in so doing, locates the research within its intellectual origins. It acts as a series of signposts that show not only the direction in which the research is going, but also where the research is coming from – its discipline area and research tradition. As such, it allows the reader to understand the approach of the research and to get some feel for the assumptions underlying the proposed investigation. As well as this, the literature review provides the opportunity to acknowledge the contribution of others and the way the current research has been influenced by the writings of other people. This is good practice and, of course, defends against accusations of plagiarism.

Identify some element of originality associated with the research

There is a general expectation that research should contain some element of originality. The spirit behind this is that there is rarely any need for research to simply replicate what has been done before. It is more worthwhile to conduct research that moves things forward. For those who are new to research, this can seem a daunting prospect. Those doing a bachelor's degree project or master's degree dissertation, for example, might wonder how they are expected to propose original research when they are yet to become experts in the area. Originality, however, is generally interpreted in a fairly broad way and in practice it tends to mean only that the proposed work is *different from* other pieces of research that already exist (Denscombe 2010). And this is one of the things that the literature review can help to demonstrate. It does not need to show that the proposed research is ground-breaking in order to contain some originality, but good research does need to contain some element that distinguishes it from research that has gone before it: something different in relation to the topic, method, theory, data, application or analysis.

Define terms and clarify concepts

The research is almost certain to involve key terms and concepts and great care should be taken to define them precisely. There should be no room for ambiguity or misunderstanding about these core ideas. The task is to identify the key terms and concepts and then pinpoint what you understand these to mean and how you will use them during the course of the research. It is good practice to show how your definitions have been drawn from the works of established authorities in the field of study. Cite the sources and explain how your particular use of the terms or concepts relates to theirs. Perhaps you wish to adopt the definition provided by a particular expert in the field. That's fine, but you must explain why you have chosen to do so. What are the strengths of the definition? Is it a standard definition in the field? Or perhaps you want to develop your own definition, in which case you need to explain why and, in doing so, refer to other possible alternatives and the reasons why you do not wish to adopt one of these.

Develop research objectives and refine research questions

Even within the confines of a research proposal, a good literature review should take the reader on a kind of intellectual journey. It should move the focus of attention from wide and general contextual issues through a review of the available literature towards specific research questions that can be investigated through empirical enquiry. Writing skills are important here in terms of being able to craft the written material in a suitable fashion.

Delimitations and scoping the research

Somewhere within any proposal the researcher needs to address the matter of *what is, and what is not, included in the research.* Sometimes this is done under a separate heading that 'delimits' the research. Sometimes it appears within the Methods section. More often than not, however, the Literature Review provides the context for researchers to establish exactly what will be included in the proposed research and what will not be included – and to justify why this is the case.

The term 'delimitations' is used in this context. To delimit means to demarcate, or to set the boundaries around something. It involves 'setting the limits'. The delimitations of a project are self-imposed boundaries decided upon by the researcher and are therefore distinct from 'limitations', which arise from factors beyond the control of the researcher. Delimitations are concerned with specifying things, such as:

- boundaries to the literature that will be *reviewed*;
- things that will be *done* in the research and things that will not be done – and why;
- items or people that will be *included* in the research and those that will not – and why;
- factors that will be *looked at* in the research and those that will not – and why;
- the time span to be *covered* – and why.

Scoping a project serves a similar purpose. Like delimitation, scoping establishes what kinds of thing are going to fall within the remit for the research and what things will not be included. It entails decisions about what the research is trying to achieve and what it is not trying to achieve, and it is a process that effectively sets boundaries around what is to be included and, importantly, what is to be excluded from the study.

These things are necessary for 'managing the expectations of stakeholders'. They spell out the *intentions behind the research* so that readers of the proposal know all they need to know about the purpose of the proposed research and its underlying premises. There are obvious benefits for the researcher in doing this. First, it helps with the planning of the research to have a clear vision of the project. Second, and equally important, it means that those who assess a proposal should not be able to misconstrue things or misunderstand what the proposed research is trying to do. The terms of reference for the proposed research are made clear through delimitations and the scoping process, and the evaluation of the proposal should be based on the premises that have been established by the researcher.

Summary of key points

A prime role of the literature review within a proposal is to construct an argument supporting the belief that the research will be *worthwhile*. The review needs to justify the proposed research by demonstrating the importance of the proposed investigation in relation to specific problems, theories, contexts, etc. Through doing this it helps the proposal in its quest to *sell an idea.*

In the context of a research proposal, the literature review is restricted by the space available and by the fact that it is likely to be a preliminary review that takes place before the start of the empirical research. It is based, therefore, on relatively few sources. These sources have to be selected carefully. They need to get the right message to the reader about the contents of the proposal and demonstrate the researcher's familiarity with the existing published work in the area. Normally they will be expected to be published sources that are authoritative and credible.

The search for relevant sources should be systematic and the process should be reported so that readers of the proposal can see how the material was identified. Initial guidance on relevant material can make use of expert advice, online searches, databases, textbooks, and review articles. Sources should be critically analysed and themes in the literature identified. The review should conclude with specific research questions that will be addressed by the research.

Writing a literature review is an iterative process – but the end-product needs to present a nice, neat logical argument supporting the choice of topic and the research questions to be investigated. To do this, a good literature review:

- refers to facts, reports, and authors to signpost the nature of the research and its purpose;
- demonstrates the researcher's familiarity with key ideas in the area of study;
- identifies the intellectual origins of the ideas underlying the proposed research;
- identifies some element of newness and originality associated with the research;
- describes the research objectives and provides a rationale for the research questions.

Finally, the literature review should establish the precise remit for the proposed research, leaving no room for ambiguity or misunderstanding. The researcher needs to define terms and be explicit about the delimitations, so that what is 'on offer' in terms of the proposed research is absolutely clear.

Further reading

Fink, A. (2010) *Conducting Research Literature Reviews: From the Internet to Paper* (3rd edn.). Thousand Oaks, CA: Sage (Chapters 1 and 5).

Hart, C. (1998*) Doing a Literature Review: Releasing the Social Science Research Imagination.* London: Sage (Chapter 1).

Machi, L. A. and McEvoy, B. T. (2009) *The Literature Review: Six Steps to Success.* Thousand Oaks, CA: Corwin Press (Chapters 3 and 5).

Ridley, D.D. (2008) *The Literature Review: A Step-by-Step Guide for Students.* London: Sage (Chapters 2, 8, and 10).

6

RESEARCH QUESTIONS

What do we need to find out?

• The importance of good research questions • The format of research questions • Types of research question • The differences between aims, research problems, objectives, and research questions • Narrowing the focus: the process of formulating a research question • The need for an open-minded approach • An example • Summary of key points • Further reading

Research questions can take the form of questions, propositions or hypotheses. These alternatives might appear to be quite different from one another, and in some respects they are. But there are three things they have in common – things that are extremely important in the context of research proposals. First, they all pose questions that are *vital for addressing the key concerns of the research*. They pinpoint exactly what the researcher needs to find out if the research is to add anything valuable to our knowledge about the topic being covered. Research questions, so to speak, 'hit the nail on the head' by asking the most pertinent questions, the most revealing questions, the most incisive questions about the issues or problems that are driving the research.

Second, whichever form they take, research questions are fairly *precise and specific*. The questions they ask are not vague or abstract. Indeed, the idea behind research questions is that they move things from the realms of the abstract to the realms of the concrete. Research questions transform the debates and ideas that have been analysed in the course of the literature review – things that might well have involved abstract concepts and general theories – and put them into a format that can be investigated empirically.

Third, research questions give an explicit vision of the kind of *data that will be collected* in the empirical phase of the research. In this respect, they occupy a pivotal position in the research proposal. They provide a conclusion to the first part of the proposal where the researcher has established the overall aims of the project and discussed what is already known in relation to the topic. And they are the starting point for the second part of the proposal that deals with the empirical investigation and how it will be conducted. They operate as the bridge between 'what we already know' and 'what we are going to look at'.

Those who evaluate research proposals will be impressed by well-formulated research questions because they will not only appreciate the information that is contained in the research questions about the direction of the research, they will also recognize that well-formulated research questions are the product of clear thinking about the proposed research. Good research questions indicate that the researcher has a good grasp of the issues and has thought carefully about the best way to approach the research. These things will enhance the prospects of success for the proposal.

> Research questions pinpoint exactly what we need to find out.

The importance of good research questions

Why are research questions considered so important for the research proposal? Bryman (2007: 5–6) states:

The research question is viewed as a crucial early step that provides a point of orientation for an investigation. It helps to link the researcher's literature review to the kinds of data that will be collected. As such, formulating a research question has an important role in many accounts of the research process as a stage that helps to militate against undisciplined data collection and analysis.

By formulating precise research questions it is possible to be more efficient in terms of the collection and analysis of data. It can save a lot of time because researchers can concentrate their efforts on things that matter. And the people who evaluate research proposals appreciate this point and will regard it as a good sign for the prospects of a successful project.

The other side of the coin is that the absence of clear research questions will be seen by readers as meaning that the ideas behind the proposed research have not been given sufficient thought or that the researcher is not really clear about how the aims of the research will be achieved. Obviously, this will not help the prospects of success. Those who evaluate the proposal will operate on the assumption that vague questions are likely to lead to vague answers – something that will undermine any idea that the proposed research could be worthwhile. They will see poorly formulated research questions as a recipe for research that will:

- waste time on meanderings up blind alleys;
- waste time on the collection of unnecessary information;
- flounder in a sea of vast quantities of issues and data;
- lead to poor quality research findings.

Top tip

Be clear in your mind about:

- what you want to investigate
- why you want to investigate it: and
- how you are going to investigate it.

(Lewis and Munn 2004: 1)

The format of research questions

What do they ask about?

Good research questions ask about things that are particularly *relevant* to the aims of the research – things that are likely to provide information that will offer some new insight relating to the aims of the research. That much has already been said. But they also ask about things that are relatively *concrete*. They avoid asking about abstract or nebulous things and focus instead on things that have substance. In the case of quantitative research, this will tend to be something that is observable or measurable. It could include questions about a particular:

- event that will be observed;
- variable that will be measured;
- indicator that will be checked;
- behaviour that will be monitored.

In the case of qualitative research, it might be something that is not directly observable. Here, the focus of the questions might be on a particular:

- belief or motive that will be interpreted;
- experience that will be described;
- attitude or opinion that will be detected;
- lifestyle or culture that will be portrayed.

Top tip

Research questions should ask about specific 'things' rather than abstract ideas. The questions should be:

- specific rather than general
- precise rather than vague
- concrete rather than abstract.

Where are they placed?

Research questions need to be justified on the basis of a *research story*. This story takes the reader on a logical journey, which narrows the focus from broad aims, through research problems or objectives, to arrive at specific research questions that can clearly be seen as addressing the aims of the research. Usually, this story unfolds during the course of the literature review, and the conclusion to a literature review will often take the form of research questions to be investigated.

Sometimes, the research questions are placed in a separate, stand-alone section of the proposal. This normally follows the literature review. And occasionally the research questions are stated within the Methods section of the proposal. But whichever position they take, the content of the questions clearly depends on the preparatory groundwork undertaken during the literature review that covers 'what we already know' and which points to 'what we need to know' in relation to the particular topic.

How are they introduced?

The introduction to the research questions should remind the reader of the way in which the list of questions has been derived from an enquiry into the available literature on the topic. For example:

> The research evidence to date suggests that (factor a) and (factor b) are important when it comes to (the topic). Bearing this in mind, this research will investigate the following research questions.

> A review of the literature indicates that there is uncertainty about the existence of (factor a) and that further information about (factor a) will be beneficial in terms of our understanding of (the topic). For this reason, the research will ask the following questions.

> Having considered the relevant and significant research and debates associated with the area, it will be valuable to conduct research into the following specific questions.

> Theories on (the topic) are divided and there is some lack of agreement about the role of (factor a) and the extent to which it is influenced by (factor b). In an effort to clarify this matter and contribute to the debate between (approach a) and (approach b), this research will investigate the following research propositions.

How many?

There are no hard and fast rules on this point. For qualitative research, it is possible that one well-constructed research question might be sufficient to specify exactly what is to be studied. Quantitative research, by contrast, can involve a list of hypotheses and alternative hypotheses that can be relatively lengthy. By way of some general guidance, however, it is quite normal for research proposals to have between three and seven research questions.

What do they look like?

Research questions can be presented as a series of bullet points or they can be listed as a sequence of statements. They are not normally embedded within a paragraph of text or merged in some other way within a larger body of text. So the first point to bear in mind about the look of research questions is that they are normally a clear, separate, and *visibly distinct component* of a research proposal.

The second point is that research questions need to work as *self-contained* items. For them to make sense, they should not make too many assumptions about what readers already know about the topic. Nor should they beg another question in response. The question 'Why is the bus system poorly managed?' is an example of a bad question in this respect. It is based on the assumption that the bus system is indeed poorly managed. Is this true? It begs the question, 'What *is* the quality of the management of the bus system?' A good research question avoids the need for any such supplementary question.

The third point is that research questions need to be *straightforward*. The questions should stick to one point and avoid combining what are really two or more separate issues within the one question – so-called 'compound' questions. Again, a poor example would be a research question along the lines, 'Why are some bus companies run efficiently and others not, and what recommendations can be made from looking at the management of profitable bus companies?' In terms of being a research question, it needs to be broken down into its component parts with each research question being both self-contained and straightforward. For example:

- What are the distinctive features of the management of bus companies that are profitable?
- In what ways, if any, do management practices in profitable bus companies differ from management practices in less successful companies?
- What elements, if any, of the management practices of profitable bus companies can be used to enhance the performance of less successful companies?

This might seem rather pedantic and long-winded compared with the original question but it is the kind of thing that is vital for the purposes of precision and clarity. It establishes distinct, stand-alone items to be investigated, dealt with one by one in order to address the overall aims of the research.

The fourth point is that research questions should be presented in a *sequential order* – logically building from one to the next. Start with the most general and move to subsidiary questions that derive from the initial one. The example above does this.

Fifth, research questions need to be framed in a way that is 'open' and that lends itself to more than one finding. They need to be genuine questions that open up the possibility of obtaining findings that run contrary to expectations. The questions should *avoid foregone conclusions*. In the example above, note the wording of the second and third questions and the way they keep things genuinely *open*. It is neither a foregone conclusion that there is any difference between profitable and less successful bus companies in terms of their management, nor is it assumed that, even if the research does reveal significant differences, these elements of good practice can be simply transplanted into the less successful companies. The questions are open.

Types of research questions

It is possible to formulate research questions in more than one way. Broadly speaking, the three options from which to choose are questions, hypotheses, and propositions. These different options tend to be associated with different styles of research and different research paradigms but as White (2009: 36) points out, broadly they serve the same purpose.

Questions

To help with formulating research questions, the best advice is to start with the standard 'Ws' – what, when, where, who. You can also add 'do' to this list even though it does not fit so neatly in an alphabetical sense! These are good for producing questions that help descriptive or exploratory research where the focus is on finding out what the situation actually is – getting to the facts of the matter. To illustrate the point, imagine a piece of research that is interested in the efficiency of public transport and, in particular, the phenomenon of clustering of buses along urban routes. (You wait for ages and then two or three buses come along together.) Initially, the research would need some evidence on which to base its conclusions. The research questions in this instance will be geared towards finding out what this situation actually is and describing things 'as they are' currently. Here, suitable research questions might take the following form:

- *What* is the frequency and extent of bunching on the bus routes?
- *When* does the bunching occur most severely during the day?
- *Where* does the bunching occur along the urban routes?
- *Who* are most affected in terms of the kinds of people using the bus route?
- *Do* bus companies currently take action to avoid bunching of buses along their routes?

Other questions lend themselves better to finding out about the causes of things and explaining why situations exist: 'why' and 'how' are valuable in this context. 'Explanatory' research questions about the bunching of buses, for example, might include:

- *Why* does the bunching of buses on urban routes occur?
- *How* can the bunching of buses be avoided?

> **Top tip**
> Keep research questions straightforward – one thing at a time.

Hypotheses

Hypotheses are the classic, scientific way of formulating a research question. In essence, hypotheses propose a *relationship* between two or more *variables*. They do so on the basis of *previous theories* and findings on the topic. And they do so in a way that is *testable*.

There are, then, four components to hypotheses, each of which deserves a little more attention. First, there is the matter of the *variables*. Hypotheses state very precisely what is going to be observed or measured. This means that for a research question to take the form of a genuine hypothesis, the subject matter to be investigated has to be of a kind that allows specific variables to be identified. Not all topics are suitable. Hypotheses are more commonly linked with the use of quantitative data and statistical analysis. However, this does not mean that they cannot be used in conjunction with qualitative research (Mason 2002; Creswell 2009). White (2009: 57) makes the point that although 'hypotheses have traditionally been linked to theory testing . . . any prediction about research findings is "hypothetical". They can be useful in many different types of study and are not just restricted to "quantitative" research or statistical analysis.'

A variable is any characteristic, quality or attribute which can vary (i.e. which can take on different values), and which can be used to distinguish between the people, the objects, or the items that are being studied.

A variable may be either quantitative or qualitative. A quantitative variable refers to a characteristic which can be measured, scored, or placed in order of magnitude (rank order), while a qualitative variable cannot be measured or expressed numerically, only classified or labelled.

(Clark 1987: 30)

Second, hypotheses predict a relationship between particular variables. It is important on this point for the hypothesis to be clear about the nature of the relationship that is being predicted. So, for example, if the variables being studied were 'bunching of buses' and 'traffic congestion', the hypothesis should be clear about whether the link will be:

- *non-directional* (bunching of buses is linked to traffic congestion) or *directional* (the extent of bunching of buses increases when the level of traffic congestion increases);

- *causal* (the bunching of buses is caused by traffic congestion) or *correlational* (the extent of bunching of buses varies in accord with the level of traffic congestion).

Third, hypotheses are based on previous theories and are logically derived from previous knowledge in the field in a very transparent manner. As Clark (1987: 30) stresses, 'An hypothesis is not merely based on guesswork, but is a tentative, carefully thought out, logical statement of a predicted outcome. It is supported by a rationale and must be consistent with existing theory.'

Fourth, hypotheses set out to test whether some relationship exists. They predict a relationship between variables in a way that can be *empirically* supported or refuted. Research hypotheses 'both indicate the question in testable form and predict the nature of the answer' (Locke et al. 2000: 14).

Following from these points, hypotheses can take the form:

If . . . (this is true as current theories suggest)

then . . . (we might expect to find the following to happen/exist)

when . . . (other factors are controlled for and certain conditions apply).

The hypothesis takes as its starting point some existing state of affairs from which it is logically possible to deduce some further expected finding, and the research sets out to compare the 'logically expected' with what is 'actually found'. So, for example, if a research project was interested in the launch of a new product (product A), the following hypothesis might be developed:

If . . . (i) consumers are motivated by self-interest, and (ii) product A offers better value for money than product B,

(two theoretical premises)

then . . . we can predict that consumers will switch from buying product B to buying product A

(expected outcome)

when . . . product A is introduced to the market and consumers have equal opportunity to purchase either brand.

(under given conditions, 'all other things being equal')

Such a statement has the virtue of being succinct and of indicating exactly what the research needs to accomplish. The research will measure the extent to which traditional purchasers of product B shift to buying product A to test whether this holds true. If it does, the findings will support the hypothesis.

Top tip

Never say that your findings will *prove* a hypothesis is correct. Results from research do not prove or disprove a hypothesis; they test the hypothesis and provide evidence that *supports* or *does not support* the hypothesis. It is important not to jump to conclusions on the basis of the findings, and the wording used to express what can and cannot be concluded from the findings is important. There is a vast philosophy of science behind the point but the basic thing to remember is that you must avoid making unwarranted claims on the basis of your findings.

Propositions

Research questions can be stated as propositions. These are declarative statements that propose things that can be checked to determine whether they hold true or not. As such, they work along the same lines as hypotheses in the sense that they formulate the research question in a way that involves a positive statement about something that the research might expect to find. Propositions, however, do not necessarily need to meet all the conditions that apply to hypotheses. They are still quite explicit about what will be focused upon during the research but they can be a bit looser than hypotheses when it comes to the way they stem from previous research, how variables will be 'measured', and how relationships will be 'tested'.

For these reasons, propositions are a useful format for research questions when researchers are investigating fairly uncharted territory and where the research evidence to date does not provide a well-established set of theories on which to base a hypothesis. A proposition can be based on more of a hunch or a bit of inspiration rather than firmly established knowledge about the topic. Continuing with the 'bunching of buses' example above, research propositions might take the form:

- Reducing traffic congestion will ease the problem of buses bunching together along urban routes.
- Styles of management influence the profitability of bus companies.

Both of these statements are testable but do not contain the specific predictions associated with a hypothesis.

The differences between aims, research problems, objectives, and research questions

The term 'research question' is occasionally used rather loosely as an umbrella term that covers a range of things concerned with the subject matter of the investigation. Aims, objectives, and research problems are all treated as falling under the broad heading of 'research questions'. However, strictly speaking, the term *research questions* should be used in a more specific way that separates its role in research proposals from that of the *aims* and the *research problems* or *objectives*.

The *aims* of the research are concerned with the direction in which the research will *go* – its targets and the benefits involved. They also indicate the scale and scope of the proposed investigation.

Link up with **Chapter 4: Aims of the Research**

The terms *research problem* and *objectives* both refer to the next level down in the processing of funnelling ideas towards research questions – a level at which the concern is primarily with what the research is trying to *do*. There is a shift in emphasis from the abstract to the concrete and an effort to translate the aims into the kind of things that have substance and which take the form of problems to be resolved, issues to be clarified, etc. This brings them in touch with research questions and, indeed, when research problems are sub-divided, 'Oftentimes, a one-to-one correspondence exists between the sub-problems and their corresponding hypotheses or questions' (Leedy and Ormrod 2004: 60).

The *research questions* show how the research will put things into practice. They specify what factors and what relationships will be investigated to provide data that will be useful in relation to the research aims and objectives. Importantly on this point, research questions should not be confused with 'data collection questions' – the kind of questions that might be asked during an interview or appear on a questionnaire. It is important to keep the distinction clear, as Gorard (2003) and White (2009) have both emphasized.

Top tip

Avoid reiterating the aims when writing the research questions. The research questions should identify specific and relevant things that will be looked at rather than broad ambitions to be aimed for.

Narrowing the focus: the process of formulating a research question

Research questions are the end-product of a process that progressively narrows the proposal's focus of interest. The process starts from the broad aims of the investigation. It then narrows down the focus to particular objectives or research problems. Finally, from these problems or objectives, research questions are formulated which pinpoint the exact things that will be investigated (see Figure 6.1).

The narrowing process

In practice, the formulation of research questions is not a one-way journey that neatly travels the logical pathway from beginning to end. There are two reasons for this. First, many people start from a position where they already have a hunch or a shrewd idea of the things they need to look at and the nature of the research problem they wish to address. Their starting point is a fair way through the 'logical' process and they are not setting out on the process with a blank sheet. Second, in reality the formulation of research questions tends to be an *iterative process* in which the eventual aims and research questions are the end-product of going back and forth, visiting and revisiting relevant ideas and issues (see Figure 6.2). The aims and the research questions are adjusted and synchronized in a sequence of modifications that take place during a protracted process of developing and refining the focus of the proposed research. It is a lot more complicated than simply starting with the aims and smoothly progressing towards the questions in a one-way, one-off fashion.

FIGURE 6.1 Narrowing the focus of research

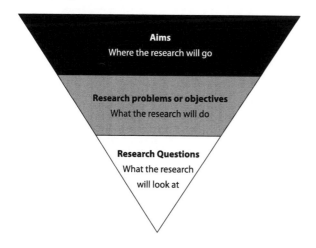

FIGURE 6.2 The iterative process of formulating research questions

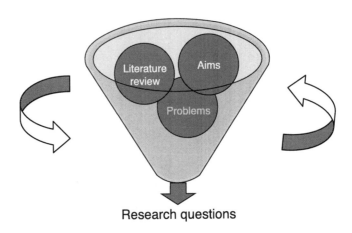

Research questions

Link up with **An iterative process**, p. 65

Neither of these points poses a major problem. It really does not matter what the starting point is, or how messy the journey towards the final research questions turns out to be, provided that two conditions are met. First, within the eventual research proposal the rationale for the questions, propositions or hypotheses must be *presented as a narrative* that is quite neat, logical, and easy to follow from the readers' point of view.

Second, the research questions that are eventually presented in the research proposal must have an obvious relevance to the aims of the research. This relevance should be made clear to the readers through the arguments developed in the Background and/or Literature Review sections of the proposal. As Figure 6.3 illustrates, the proposal needs to present a vision of the research as one that stems from a broad area of interest but which then focuses on increasingly specific things, arriving at the research questions which pinpoint the exact indicators that will be looked at.

> **Top tip**
> Research questions are not the same as aims. When writing research questions, avoid simply reiterating the aims. Commit yourself to the investigation of specific, relevant factors that will provide useful information.

FIGURE 6.3 Developing research questions – narrowing the focus

		Example	Comment
AREA		Employment and work motivation	General area of interest (e.g. a sub-area of a discipline, or a work-related concern)
TOPIC		Absence from work	Specific topic of concern from within the general area
LITERATURE REVIEW		Absence rates are related to pay and job satisfaction as well as other factors, such as job security, work conditions, health and safety at work, worker morale, career and promotions	What is already known about the topic? Background research to identify the key issues and existing knowledge about the topic
RESEARCH AIMS		To investigate how rates of absenteeism are linked with levels of pay and levels of job satisfaction	These are statements about the general purpose of the research. They are relatively non-specific, abstract indications of where the research is
		To gauge how far rates of absenteeism can be reduced through changes to the pay structure and changes to levels of job satisfaction	going – its ambitions, its targets, its *goals*
		To explore the link between these factors in the context of lower-paid workers	It is 'all about' absenteeism, pay and job satisfaction
RESEARCH OBJECTIVES		To apply existing knowledge about the relationship between rates of absenteeism and levels of pay and job satisfaction to the specific situation of low-paid workers in the UK retail sector with a view to finding appropriate means for reducing absenteeism	Here is a statement about what the research will *do*
			It will use existing knowledge, *apply* it to a particular context, and *develop* new knowledge that can have a practical value
		To focus on employees in three case study companies as a good example from which to draw more general conclusions	
RESEARCH QUESTIONS		Is there a statistical correlation between levels of pay and absenteeism among employees working for the three case study retailers?	These are the questions that the research will actually *ask* to find out what it wants to know
		What is the profile of employees working in the shops (age, sex, etc.)?	They focus on specific *key indicators* and *relevant factors* on which information is needed
		Do certain kinds of worker have higher absenteeism rates than others?	
		Are certain kinds of employees more frustrated by their work role than others, and is this correlated with a tendency to take days off work?	
		What reasons do employees give for being absent from work?	
		What aspirations do the shop workers have in terms of intrinsic rewards from the job and career progression?	
		To what extent is job satisfaction related to levels of pay?	

Narrowing focus

The need for an open-minded approach

The point has been made above that research questions need to be phrased in such a way that the findings can either support or challenge any expectations the researchers might initially hold. Whether constructed as questions, hypotheses or propositions, they need to be phrased in a way that offers a genuine chance of finding the unexpected. They should never pre-empt findings or suggest in any way that the findings are a foregone conclusion. Even when hypotheses and propositions posit a relationship that might be expected to exist, they do so in the spirit of an open-minded approach whose purpose is to check whether a particular finding occurs rather than presume it will exist.

This is more than just a matter of wording. It is an important aspect of research thinking that research is conducted to check and test our expectations rather than to confirm what we already know. Researchers need to approach things with a genuine spirit of discovery and exploration in which they recognize that what they thought was true might not necessarily be borne out by the findings of their research. Researchers have to be open to the possibility of being wrong, of finding the unexpected, of discovering something new – and the wording of the research questions should reflect this.

Qualitative research and grounded theory approaches

There are types of qualitative research that have a particular concern about open-mindedness. *Exploratory research*, which sets out to describe things (e.g. types of ethnography and types of phenomenology) or to discover things (e.g. grounded theory) can sometimes take the position that researchers should start with a completely open mind about what will be found by the investigation and that researchers should not have their open minds tainted by prior expectations derived from reading previous work on the topic. The worry is that if researchers use existing theories as the basis for producing research questions, this will create a mental straitjacket that will constrain their thinking and cloud their minds. It will stop them from 'seeing' things afresh and seeing things 'as they really are'.

In the context of writing successful research proposals, there are two points that are worth making about this approach. The first is that it is a fairly radical position to take and it is also controversial. This does not make it 'wrong' – and this is not the context to engage in a discussion of the epistemological merits of such a stance on research – but it does mean that it is not a stance that is likely to be shared by the vast majority of those evaluating research proposals. Right or wrong, the practical reality is that the chances of a research proposal being approved are very slim if it says: 'I will approach the study with a completely open mind and will therefore not read previous work on the topic and will not have specific research questions before I begin the research.' The second point is that exploratory qualitative research can generally manage to get a suitable balance between the need to 'see things afresh' and the need to start research with some form of research questions in mind. Indeed, there is a definite need for qualitative research to do so. As Marshall and Rossman (1999: 38) state:

> The proposal should be sufficiently clear both in research questions and design so that the reader can evaluate its do-ability; on the other hand, the proposal should reserve the flexibility that is the hallmark of qualitative methods. This suggests that the research questions should be general enough to permit exploration but focussed enough to delimit the study. Not an easy task.

To accomplish this balancing act, the proposal is more likely to formulate its research questions in the form of statements than hypotheses or propositions, and the statements themselves are likely to be relatively general. As Creswell recommends, they should take the form of a central question followed by associated sub-questions that narrow the focus of the research and which, keeping within the spirit of emergent research designs, should start with appropriate verbs. Cresswell (2003: 106) suggests the following possibilities:

- Discover . . . (e.g. grounded theory)
- Seek to understand . . . (e.g. ethnography)
- Explore a process . . . (e.g. case study)
- Describe the experiences . . . (e.g. phenomenology)
- Report the stories . . . (e.g. narrative research).

An example: research on the distribution of bakery products

In the example below, imagine that the researcher wishes to investigate transportation issues, specifically those relating to the delivery of bakery products. The researcher is approaching the topic in a way that draws on two 'disciplines': management practice and transport logistics. These two strands will provide the starting points for reviewing the literature and for getting a feel for the theories and practical concerns that are important for getting a good understanding of the topic. A review of the literature might well reveal that two factors are particularly important: the costs of transport and the punctuality of deliveries. The nature of bakery products with relatively small profit margins and a particularly short shelf life makes these two factors important for the commercial survival of bakery companies. The researcher has limited time and resources to conduct the research and, in light of this, opts to conduct a case study of a company where the researcher already has personal contacts – Broadbread Ltd. In the proposal produced by the researcher, the research questions could be presented as questions, hypotheses or propositions depending on the kind of research that is to be carried out and the kind of research tradition from which the researcher comes. Some indication of what these might look like is provided in Table 6.1. But whatever approach is taken, note how:

- the research questions *link to the aims* and the objectives, and
- the research questions involve specific *factors that are to be 'looked at'* in order to meet the aims of the research.

Table 6.1 Research questions – an example

Topic	The distribution of bakery products	Comments
Aims	To evaluate transport logistics in relation to the delivery of bakery products To identify elements of 'good practice' that can be applied at an industry-wide level To make recommendations for reducing the costs of delivering bakery products and improving the punctuality of deliveries to local stores	*This indicates* what *the research will be about and* why *it should be worthwhile* *The aims explain where the research is going and what its targets are*
Objectives	*To do this, the research will:* Describe and analyse existing delivery practices at Broadbread Ltd. Compare practices at Broadbread Ltd. with best practice in the transport industry Examine the key cost components influencing vehicle purchasing in the company Identify the main causes of delays in the delivery schedule	*This identifies what the particular areas of investigation will be* *The objectives point to what the research will actually do*
Research questions . . .		
as Questions	1. What are the main factors disrupting the punctual delivery of the bakery products? 2. How frequently do delays occur in the delivery of bakery products to local stores in East Anglia? 3. What measures are taken at Broadbread Ltd. to deal with the occurrence of delays? 4. What proportion of Broadbread's annual budget is spent on the purchase of new delivery vehicles? 5. Are there particular features of Broadbread's transport management that can be held responsible for delays in deliveries?	*The questions focus on key factors that need to be investigated* *They do not rely entirely on existing theories and allow for exploration of new factors*

Topic	The distribution of bakery products	Comments
as Hypotheses	1. If management fails to take advantage of transport logistics software and if costs/delays continue at current rates, then Broadbread Ltd. will lose 12% of its market share within the next two years 2. If industry best practice with respect to transport management is implemented at Broadbread Ltd., then this will lead to a 10% improvement in the punctuality of deliveries to local stores 3. If leasing agreements replace current purchasing and maintenance arrangements at Broadbread Ltd., then overall transports costs will be reduced by 15%, all other things being equal	*Hypotheses involve specific predictions about the result of introducing new factors They rely on detailed knowledge and are based heavily on well-established theories*
as Propositions	1. Management practices at Broadbread Ltd. do not accord with current best practice in the industry 2. Cost savings can be made through changes to company policy relating to vehicle purchasing 3. The punctuality of deliveries can be improved by the use of transport logistics software to reduce the impact of predictable and avoidable delays	*Propositions assert a fact which the research can proceed to investigate to see if it is supported by the evidence The predictions are less specific than those associated with hypotheses*

Summary of key points

Well-formulated research questions improve the prospects of the proposal being successful. They are likely to impress those who evaluate the proposal because they reflect a good degree of precision in the researcher's thinking and planning about the research. Equally, the absence of crisp, precise research questions will jeopardize the research proposal's chances of success because evaluators will regard it as evidence of fuzzy thinking or poor preparation for the project.

Research questions can take the form of questions, propositions or hypotheses, depending on the style of research that is being used. Whatever their form, they should tell the reader of the proposal what the research is going to *look at*. The things that will be 'looked at' need to fit two criteria. They need to be:

- *relevant*: the literature review should have been used to identify what factors can be used as relevant in relation to the aims of the research;
- *specific*: in the case of quantitative data, this is something that is observable or measurable; in the case of qualitative research, it is something that can be described or interpreted.

Whatever form they take, research questions should be clear and concise. Good research questions:

- are *apparent* as a distinct feature within the research proposal;
- are *self-contained*: they do not combine questions or include questions that beg other questions, nor do they make unwarranted presumptions;
- are *straightforward*: each question/proposition/hypothesis deals with a distinct issue or idea – one sentence, one issue;
- *avoid foregone conclusions*: they should be 'open' and not presume an outcome;
- are presented in a *logical sequence*.

Within research proposals, research questions are normally presented as the end-product of a 'funnelling' process in which there is a narrowing of focus from aims through to objectives and finally to research questions.

Further reading

Andrews, R. (2003) *Research Questions*. London: Continuum (Chapters 2, 3, and 6).

Campbell, J.P., Daft, R.L. and Hulin, C.L. (1982) *What to Study: Generating and Developing Research Questions*. Beverly Hills, CA: Sage.

Creswell, J.W. (2009) *Research Design: Qualitative, Quantitative, and Mixed Methods Approaches* (3rd edn.). Thousand Oaks, CA: Sage (Chapter 7).

Fraenkel, J., Wallen, N. and Hyun, H. (2011) *How to Design and Evaluate Research in Education* (6th edn.). New York: McGraw-Hill (Chapters 2 and 3).

Kumar, R. (2010) *Research Methodology: A Step-by-Step Guide for Beginners* (3rd edn.). London: Sage (Chapters 4, 5, 6, and 13).

White, P. (2009) *Developing Research Questions: A Guide for Social Scientists*. Basingstoke: Palgrave Macmillan (Chapters 2–4).

7

RESEARCH METHODS

How will we get the necessary information?

AIMS
What is it
all about?

LIT REVIEW
What do we
already know?

OUTCOMES
What will be
the benefits

Research
proposals

RESEARCH QUESTIONS
What do we need
to find out?

ETHICS
Is the research
socially acceptable?

METHODS
How will we get the
necessary information?

RESOURCES
How long will it take
and what will it cost?

> • *Description of the methods* • *Justification of the choice of
> methods* • *Risk assessment* • *Limitations* • *Summary of key points*
> • *Further reading*

By the time readers reach this section of the proposal, they should have a clear idea of what the research will attempt to do and they will hopefully be persuaded that this is a worthwhile venture. They will now want to know more about how the research is to be conducted and their attention will shift from *what* is to be studied to *how* it will be investigated.

There will be a number of questions in their minds but these essentially boil down to three basic issues. First, *what methods will be used*? Readers will want to know 'in a nutshell':

- What research strategy will be used?
- What kind of data will be collected, and how much?
- How will the data be collected?
- Who, or what, will be included?
- How will the data be analysed?

Once they are clear on these they can then turn their attention to the second issue. They will want to know *why the methods have been chosen* and why the research will be done in the way that has been outlined. They will want to know:

- Are the proposed methods suitable and likely to produce worthwhile data?

The third and final issue readers will be concerned with is *whether the proposed methods can be implemented*. They will want to be assured at a practical level that the proposed methods can be carried out successfully and will ask:

- Will the methods work and are they feasible?

Reflecting these concerns, the Methods section of a research proposal tends to break down into two parts. The first part sets out to provide the reader with the facts about what will be done. The second part attempts to demonstrate that the actions and choices outlined in the first part will be appropriate and are justifiable – that they are 'good' in terms of the overall aims of the research, and that they are practical.

Description of the methods

In the context of a research proposal there should be no chance of any confusion about what is on offer and an outline of the methods 'up front' serves to eliminate the prospects of any uncertainty or ambiguity from the reader's point of view about what the methods will involve. At the beginning of the Methods section, then, there should be a straightforward description of the methods and the data that will be collected. This should be a *matter of fact* assertion about what will be done. At this point there should be no attempt to justify the methods – the point is simply to inform the readers so that they can better understand the situation. Justifications come later.

The statement should be *brief*. There is little scope for wasted words or the inclusion of irrelevant items. The information that is given to the readers needs to be enough for them to understand the proposed methods but nothing more. Remember, *a research proposal is not an essay*. It is an outline plan of action that provides the reader with the information they require – no more, no less.

> A good, crisp outline of the methods is important not just because of the information it provides, but also of the impression it conveys. It says to the reader: 'I know exactly what I am doing in this research project', and this is likely to make the reader feel confident about the quality of the research design that is about to be unfolded in the subsequent parts of the Methods section of the proposal.

What research strategy will be used?

The description of the methods should start with a clear statement about the approach that is to be adopted. It is good practice to specify which *research strategy* will be used – whether the research will be based on a survey or a case study, whether it will use experiments or do ethnography, whether it will use grounded theory or involve mixed methods, and so on. This can be dealt with by statements such as: 'This research will use a case study approach to delve deeply into . . . (the research questions)' or 'This research will adopt a mixed methods strategy that combines a survey approach and case study approach to explore . . . (the research questions).'

What methods of data collection will be used?

Attention should then be placed on the tools used to collect the data. Some commonplace options from which to choose include:

- *Interview*: will the research use unstructured, semi-structured or structured types of interview?
- *Questionnaire*: will the questionnaire use open-ended or closed-ended questions? Or will it include both?
- *Observation*: will the research involve systematic observation or participant observation? What items will be observed?

- *Documents*: will the research focus on documents – diaries, websites, minutes of meetings, official records, etc.?

What kind of data will be collected?

The next thing that is required is a description of exactly what kind of data will be collected. It is useful, therefore, to be explicit about whether the research will use *quantitative or qualitative data* – will the research rely on one or other, or will it adopt a mixed methods approach?

How much data will be collected?

The amount of data to be collected should be specified in a positive and confident manner. It should be based on anticipated numbers and should avoid any sense of uncertainty or vagueness in the way the details are presented. There are two reasons for this. First, the readers need to get a reasonably clear picture in their minds about the scale and scope of the investigation. They can do this on the basis of actual numbers that are given but will struggle to do so if they are given only vague and woolly descriptions of amounts such as 'a large number of', 'many', 'few', 'some', etc. Second, tentative statements which state that the research 'hopes' to collect a certain volume of data or which 'might' manage to obtain a stated amount of data send the wrong message. They suggest a lack of confidence, hesitance about what is being proposed. They convey a sense of doubt – which is definitely the wrong message in terms of being able to persuade the readers that the research methods are workable and good.

Link up with **Precision**, p. 47

What are needed, instead, are bold statements that quantify the amount of data, statements such as:

Questionnaires will be distributed to 430 employees of the Broadbread bakery company. With an anticipated response rate of 30 per cent, this will provide 129 completed questionnaires available for analysis.

The research will commence with five lone-parents who have direct experience of raising children who suffer from eating disorders. Using snowball sampling it is anticipated that the total number of parents interviewed will be 30.

However, being so precise about the numbers will worry some people, who might ask: 'How can I know exactly how many responses I will get to my survey?', 'How do I know in advance how many people I will need to interview as part of my qualitative research?, or 'What happens if in practice I don't manage to get the amount of data I said I would?'

These are reasonable questions to pose, and should not be dismissed lightly. After all, researchers need to be honest when they produce a proposal and they need to be aware that proposals can involve a sense of contractual obligation in which there is a 'promise' to deliver what is being offered. It is important to recognize these points and uphold the principle of honesty in a proposal. However, the figures that are provided about the amount of data to be collected and analysed can be regarded more as *targets* than as promises. No-one will be too worried if a proposal says that it will conduct fifty interviews and ends up actually only doing forty-five. This is no major sin. On the other hand, if the proposal indicated that it would collect 1000 questionnaire responses but, in the event, collected just 100, then this is a serious deviation from what was 'offered' and it would bring into question the integrity of the researcher and the proposal.

> **Top tip**
> Indicate target figures you believe you can obtain.

Who (or what) will be included?

The people or things to be included in the research need to be identified with a good degree of precision. This is another key component of the information that readers will need to evaluate the overall value of the proposed research. First, it calls upon the researcher to be absolutely clear about the *research population*. The Methods section of the proposal, perhaps reiterating information provided in the Background section, should pinpoint exactly which people or things are the object of the research. The research population might be, for instance:

- an occupational group (such as 'supply teachers in secondary education' or 'air force recruits');
- a demographic group (such as 'teenagers' or 'pensioners');
- an organization (such as 'dental practices' or 'high street banks');
- a kind of event (such as 'redundancies' or 'visits');
- a type of item (such as 'collectables' or 'computers').

In all likelihood, the research population will involve a combination of two or more of such categories. So, drawing from the list above, the research population might be 'pensioners who visit high street banks' or 'supply teachers in secondary education facing redundancy'.

Second, researchers need to be explicit about their *selection of items* (people or things) to be included in the research. Where the research population is fairly small, the researcher might choose to include *all* of the people or things in the study. This needs to be stated. However, for most research, even small-scale research, the selection of participants tends to be based on some form of *sampling*. And this, likewise, needs to be stated: how will the researcher choose among the overall research population who to include in the study and who to leave out?

A simple statement about the selection of participants will refer to the size of the sample. This would be along the lines of 'The research will be based on a 10 per cent sample of all air force recruits joining the force during a 12-month period.' This is okay as far as it goes, but any statement about the selection of participants really needs to include information about *how* the selection will be undertaken as well. If there is to be a 10 per cent sample, then how will that 10 per cent be chosen? Readers need to know. They need to be supplied with information not just about the sample size but also about the *sampling technique*. It should be clear whether the selection is to be done on the basis of random sampling, quota sampling or purposive sampling. If it is random sampling, for example, there needs to be more information telling the reader whether it will be systematic random sampling, cluster sampling, stratified sampling or whatever. The important point to bear in mind is that a word or two specifying the exact sampling technique that will be used can have a huge impact on the credibility of the proposal.

Top tip
Clearly state which sampling technique will be used in the research.

How will the data be collected?

The practicalities of collecting the data are important. They are not a mundane backdrop to the proposal but a core feature of the Methods section, and the information supplied about how the data will be collected can make the difference between whether a project is deemed feasible or not by those evaluating it.

When describing how the data will be collected the first thing to bear in mind is that simply stating which method(s) will be used does not really go far enough in terms of giving the reader the necessary insight about the practicalities. Stating which method(s) will be used is vital, of course, but as was noted in connection with sampling, it is not really sufficient to leave things at that. The same method can require different means of data acquisition, and this has a direct bearing on issues relating to whether the data collection will be feasible. So, with:

- *interviews*, will they be face-to-face, one-to-one, via telephone, focus group? Will interviews be recorded?
- *questionnaires*, will they be administered to groups or to individuals? Will they be paper/optical mark recognition questionnaires or will they be online web-based versions? Will they use open- or closed-ended questions?
- *observations*, will the data be based on field notes, contemporary notes or an observation schedule?
- *documents*, will they be official documents or informal records? Will they consist of text or images? Will they be online documents like websites or paper-based archive material?

An account of how the data will be collected should also include some indication of the schedule for the research. Simple and straightforward information can be very effective in this respect. In just a few words, this part of the proposal can tell the reader:

- when the data will be collected (month and year);
- how long data collection will continue (duration of research);
- where the data will be collected (location, situation).

Top tip

Provide details of how and when the methods will be put into practice. A good proposal does not rely on a simple statement of which method (or methods) will be used. It complements this with additional information about the particular variant of the method and how the method will be used.

Access and authorization

In many respects, this is an integral part of the issue about how the data will be collected. It is so important, though, that it warrants consideration under a separate heading. What any evaluator of a research proposal will know is that unless you can get access to the necessary sources of data, a research project will be doomed. In fact, it will not take place. Access to the necessary sources of data is absolutely essential for any project.

Experienced researchers realize that access to the data is not something that can be taken for granted. It takes a lot of forethought. It can depend on personal contacts and networks. And it can cost money. So the kind of questions in the back of the minds of the people who evaluate the proposal will include:

- Will the research need specialist equipment for this research? Will the funds be available to pay for the use of this equipment, and has the researcher been trained in its use?
- Has the researcher got the appropriate personal credentials and skills to allow them to conduct the investigation?
- Who needs to authorize access to the settings, organizations, and people and how likely is it that such authorization will be granted?
- Can access to the data be achieved through legitimate and legal means?

Readers will be looking for the kinds of statements that will persuade them that access to the data will *not* pose a practical problem when it comes to undertaking the research. Here are some examples of the kind of statements that work well.

Access to people and organizations
Head teachers at the twelve schools have been contacted and eight have so far agreed to allow their schools to be used in the research, subject to the consent of participating teachers and students.

Company directors at the firm have agreed in principle to the research and have authorized the use of the employees' email addresses for making contact to arrange interviews.

Access to events and settings
The researcher is a qualified nurse working within the hospital and will be able to observe and record the activities within the ward as part of her routine managerial duties.

Access to equipment
The specialized equipment for data collection is available within the laboratory. A training course will be attended and the equipment will be booked for use during the period of research.

Access to documents and records
The research will use archive data that is freely available in the public domain.

Top tip

Explain how you will gain access to key sources of data. The onus is on the researcher to persuade the readers of the proposal that access will not be a problem, and a few well-chosen words in this respect can greatly benefit the proposal's prospects of success.

How will the data be analysed?

The proposal should say how the data will be analysed. There needs to be a brief description of how the researcher proposes to make sense of the data that will be collected, the processes or techniques involved and, where appropriate, some reference to the software program that will be used. This applies as much to the analysis of qualitative data as it does to quantitative data. The information allows the reader to decide whether the techniques of analysis are appropriate and this, of course, will have a strong bearing on the overall evaluation of the proposal.

In the case of quantitative data, the proposal needs to state whether the analysis will be based on frequency counts (using, for example, contingency tables and bar charts) or whether some statistical analysis of the data will take place. It might well involve both, of course. If statistical analysis is to be involved, the technique should be named (e.g. chi-square test, Pearson correlation, linear regression). Experienced readers of proposals will be looking so see that treatment of the data is suitable, bearing in mind the nature of the quantitative data that will be collected (e.g. nominal, ordinal or interval data). And then the software program that will be used to conduct the statistical analysis can be named. This is not really vital, but it is common to find reference to the use of Stata, SPSS, Excel or similar software.

With qualitative data there is as much need to be specific about the process of analysis as there is with quantitative data. Where the analysis involves inter-pretation, which is the kind of analysis that tends to be more commonly associated with the notion of qualitative data, then readers need to be told about *how* the data will be interpreted – about the process and techniques used in the development of codes, categories, and concepts (e.g. open coding, axial coding). They need to be informed about the use of memos and research diaries as aids to the interpretation of the data. They should get information about how relationships between codes will be established, and about how the emerging themes will be checked back against the data (e.g. constant comparative method, respondent validation). Computer software is increasingly being seen as an essential tool in the analysis of qualitative data and, for this reason, it is quite important to identify the software package to be used (e.g. NVivo, MAXQDA, Atlas.ti).

> **Top tip**
> Indicate how you plan to analyse the data. This applies to qualitative as much as it does to quantitative research.

Example 1
A survey approach will be used for this research. The research population will be all students enrolled in Years 10 and 11 of schools in the county of

Easthamptonshire. A cluster sampling technique will be used that will include all Year 10 and 11 students attending four schools in the county ($n = 800$). A questionnaire will be piloted and then distributed during routine lesson time to all students in the sample. The survey will include questions on the ten factors identified through the literature review as likely to have an impact on smoking behaviour. Regression analysis will be used on the quantitative data from the survey (using the Stata software program). The research has been approved in principle by the local authority and the head teachers of the schools. It will be conducted during the months of May and June 20xx.

Example 2
The research will use a case study approach. This will enable exploratory research into the meaning of loyalty for employees faced with reduced hours and short-term lay-offs during a period of economic recession. The case study organization, Company A, is typical of large-scale manufacturing companies hit by a downturn in demand for car components. The human resources department is supporting the research and providing access to staff names and work-based email addresses. A mixed methods approach will be adopted combining qualitative data from interviews with quantitative data from an online questionnaire survey of company employees. Systematic random sampling will be used to select 30 employees for the interviews and 400 employees for the questionnaire. A response rate of 25 per cent will provide 100 completed questionnaires. Research will be conducted on site over a six-month period. Interviews will be transcribed and used as the basis for a narrative analysis. Data from the questionnaires will be analysed on the basis of themes emerging from the interviews (using t-test and chi-square). NVivo and SPSS software will be used. Research will commence in Sept 20xx and data collection will take place over a three-month period.

Example 3
The research will use a quasi-experimental approach to evaluate the impact of an intervention aimed at improving physical fitness among nurses. Research will be conducted with male and female nurses at one hospital in the Northwest region of the country. A representative sample of 100 nurses will be sought based on sex, age, and body mass index. Quantitative measures of their physical fitness will be taken before and after the intervention. Participants will be randomly allocated to an experimental group and a control group: equal numbers in each. The experimental group will engage in a four-month intervention programme involving 20 minutes a day spent doing a treadmill exercise. Comparison of findings between the experimental group and the control group will take place after four months. Logistic regression will be used to adjust for other relevant factors such as the nurses' marital status, working hours,

involvement in sports or other regular exercise. Preliminary approval for the research has been obtained in writing from the director of nursing at the hospital.

Checklist for the description of the methods

Have I included brief information about:

- approach/strategy?
- kind of data (qualitative/quantitative/mixed method, choice of method)?
- how much data?
- who (or what) will be included, and how selected?
- how the data will be collected (when, where, practicalities)?
- access to data and authorization?
- data analysis (process and techniques)?

Justification of the choice of methods

The second component to the methods section explains *why* the proposed methods have been chosen. Its purpose is to justify the choices that have been made and to persuade the reader that the proposed methods will not only work, but work well. It is normally longer than the previous section, describing which methods will be used, and it provides an opportunity for the researcher to go into a bit more depth. References to relevant methodological sources should be included in this section because these can be powerful allies in the effort to address the kind of questions that those who evaluate the proposal will have in their mind. Such questions include:

- Will the methods produce data that are relevant for addressing the research questions?
- Are the methods the best available under the circumstances? Are there better alternatives?
- Will the methods work? Will they do the job?

More detail

There are a number of crucial decisions about the approach to a piece of research that are not automatically communicated by broad umbrella terms such as 'survey' or 'experiment' or other such names of general research strategies. Often, they leave questions about the approach unanswered, including:

- *Cross-sectional or longitudinal time frame*: Will the data come from a snapshot of things on one occasion, or will they follow the development of things over time? Or will the research combine the two?
- *Present, past or comparative data*: Will the data be based on the present day, will the research use historical data, or will it compare instances across societies or over time?
- *Large numbers or small numbers*: Will the data involve large numbers or will the data stem from focused study on a small number of instances?
- *Controlled environment or natural event*: Will the data be produced in a controlled environment such as a laboratory, or will the data be gathered 'in the field' in naturally occurring situations? Or will the research combine both?
- *Exploratory or explanatory research*: Will the research look at new and fairly under-researched topics to describe matters and discover new things, or will it build on a well-developed body of knowledge to explain why things happen and what their underlying causes are?

This list gives an indication of the kind of further information that can be included in the justifications section. It is not an exhaustive list, and it shouldn't be treated as a checklist because it might not be necessary to incorporate each and every dimension into the discussion.

Alternative possibilities

When writing a research proposal, the researcher needs to be conscious that there are likely to be alternative ways of doing things, each with its own strengths and weaknesses, and thus the success of the research proposal will owe a great deal to how well the researcher *justifies* his or her choice of methods. The point is that writing a successful proposal depends not just on selecting a suitable method but also on arguing that this has advantages compared with other possibilities when it comes to producing data that is useful for addressing the aims of the research.

Top tip

Show how the chosen method is preferable to potential alternatives. Discuss their respective merits and failings.

Methods as 'fit for purpose'?

How, then, can the choice of methods be justified? Well, one fairly straightforward way to tackle this is to use the *Checklist for Methods* (above) and consider the merits of the various components in terms of:

- their suitability for the research questions;
- their implications for the quality of the data.

Obviously, within the confines of a research proposal it is not possible to write a full essay providing a justification of the methods. Space constraints force the researcher to be selective about where to place the emphasis. But, by way of guidance, the discussion could focus on issues such as the following:

- The use of *qualitative or quantitative data*: What are their respective strengths? Which is better suited to the needs of this particular research? Is a mixed-methods approach preferable?
- *Depth or breadth* of data: Will a case study be better than a survey, or vice versa, in terms of the particular research questions being looked at? Is there a need for depth of focus or is there a need for data drawn from widespread sources?
- The *validity* of the data produced: Will the data be accurate? Will they focus on the right issues? Is the chosen method better than alternatives in terms of getting honest responses from participants?
- The *reliability* of the method: Will the method(s) produce the same data if the same research is repeated?
- The possibility of *generalizing* from the findings: Can the findings be extrapolated to other situations/examples? Is this possible and is it important? Is this crucial for the research?
- The extent to which the data are *representative*: Is it better to include all (or a sample) of a population or will research along the lines of a case study be more suitable? Are data based on extreme examples or special instances more *valuable*?
- The extent to which the methods are *objective*: Is this possible bearing in mind the research questions being addressed? How much does it matter?

Risk assessment

It is good practice to undertake some form of risk assessment in connection with a research proposal. Occasionally, this might need to be a fairly formal procedure involving scrutiny of the proposed plan of research by a designated person or committee. This is more likely when the research is large-scale in nature or if it involves research in the areas of health (e.g. medicine, nursing) or biotechnology. In the case of proposals linked with small-scale research for bachelor's degree projects, master's degree dissertations or PhD degree applications, a risk assessment is far more likely to be something conducted 'internally' by the researcher who will reflect on the relevant risks as a part of his or her work towards writing the proposal. Even when an external body does not conduct a formal risk assessment, however, it is important to *show* that careful thought has been given to the matter.

Top tip

It needs to be evident to the readers that a risk assessment has been carried out.

In the context of the Methods section of a research proposal, the key purpose of a risk assessment is to identify factors that might have a negative impact on the prospects of completing the project. Having identified such factors, it then becomes easier to think ahead and to plan ways of preventing them from occurring or, at least, ameliorating their effects. This will enhance the prospects of the research being successfully completed.

Among the range of risks to be considered one of the most significant is the risk posed by *unexpected events*. Of course, a well-planned piece of research should aim to minimize the prospects of unexpected events arising which can threaten the completion of the project. In practice, however, it is not always possible to entirely eliminate the occurrence of unexpected and unwanted events. Things sometimes happen that have the potential to knock the project off course, to cause delays or, worst of all, to lead to the failure of the project to meet its objectives. The question 'What if . . .?' comes into play a lot in this connection:

- What if I am refused access to the organization and cannot get the data?
- What if new policies are put in place that change the situation?
- What if the funding for use of equipment dries up before I have completed the research?

The people who evaluate research proposals will want to see that some consideration has been given to the kind of events that could pose a threat to the survival of the project. They will be looking for evidence that, on the basis of a risk assessment, the design of the research:

- goes some way to eliminating the most obvious risks;
- has contingency plans for those risks that cannot be eliminated;
- involves enough flexibility to survive if problems arise.

Top tip

Think about things that might go wrong – and how to avoid them.

Link up with **Risk assessment**, p. 131

Limitations

The Limitations section of a research proposal is concerned with what can, and what cannot, be concluded on the basis of the proposed research. It incorporates caveats about the findings from the research and how they can be used, and it guides readers towards an appropriate understanding of the limits of the research. The Limitations section can appear as a stand-alone section of the proposal, or as a sub-section of the Methods section.

When researchers identify the limitations to their research they are not simply being modest about the potential achievements of the project. Neither are they setting out to 'rubbish' their own work by highlighting all the weaknesses and flaws they can think of relating to the proposal. This, after all, might persuade the reader that the research is not going to be worthwhile! No – what the researchers are actually trying to do is to *provide a measured, balanced appraisal of what the research can do bearing in mind its particular design, its methods, and its scope.*

Being open and honest about such limitations sends the correct signals to those who evaluate proposals. No research is perfect and any research that does not recognize its own weaknesses (as well as its strengths) will be deluded. It is worrying to evaluators if they do not see the researcher clearly acknowledging the limitations to the research, because it could be inferred that the researcher is rather naive or even ignorant about the implications of the research that is being proposed.

Top tip

Be open about the limitations of the proposed research. All research has its limitations.

What kind of things should be included in the Limitations section? In general, the things that warrant attention are:

- limitations associated with the methods; and
- limitations caused by circumstances beyond the control of the researcher.

Approaches and methods each have their respective strengths and weaknesses and the Limitations section of the proposal provides a setting for acknowledging any relevant limitations associated with the particular methods that have been chosen for the research. So, for example, if a case study approach has been chosen this part of the proposal gives an opportunity to pre-empt likely qualms some readers might have about how far it is possible to generalize from the research findings. If a questionnaire survey is to be used the Limitations section might be the time to acknowledge that questionnaires do not provide the kind of depth of data that an interview method would deliver. The point is not to write an essay on the respective pros and cons of alternative methods but to briefly point out any aspects of the research design that have limitations with respect to the purpose of the specific piece of research that is being proposed. This might include such things as:

- limits to how far the findings lend themselves to being generalized to other situations/examples;
- limits to the possibility of checking the accuracy of findings;
- limits to the ability to confirm that data comes from a representative sample of the research population;
- limits to objectivity resulting from the role of the researcher in data collection and analysis.

There are also limitations that stem from circumstances beyond the control of the researcher and these, too, require consideration within the proposal. Such limitations reflect the fact that research does not take place in an ideal world where researchers are able to decide for themselves exactly what data they need and how they will be collected. In the real world of doing research, there are practical factors that need to be taken into account that inevitably shape the way that the research can be conducted. Things that are routinely referred to in this respect are:

- restricted access to significant sources of data;
- restrictions arising from the resources available (time and money);
- limits to the sample size.

Note how these things are different from *de*limitations, where the restrictions stem from decisions and choices taken deliberately by the researcher. Delimitations concern choices under the control of the researcher, whereas limitations relate to 'external' factors over which the researcher does not have control.

The point of airing these concerns is to acknowledge the ways in which knowledge produced by the research will need to be interpreted cautiously. Its purpose, in a sense, is to warn readers of the dangers of jumping to unwarranted conclusions on the basis of the evidence that is presented to them.

> **Top tip**
>
> Limitations should not imply that an alternative research design would be better. Do not imply that you may have made a poor choice of design or methods. All things considered, they should be defended as the best choice possible.

Other considerations

The justification of the methods can go beyond these matters. There are, indeed, three further things that are highly relevant:

- research ethics
- data protection
- risk assessment.

Sometimes these are incorporated into the broader discussion of the methods. In this book, however, they are treated as separate items and considered separately in Chapter 9.

Summary of key points

The Methods section of a research proposal does two things. First, it provides information on how the data will be collected. This section is brief, precise, and to the point. In positive tones, it should give a factual description of *what, when, and where* the data are to be collected. This should include:

- the research *strategy* to be used;
- the *kind of data* to be collected;
- the *selection procedure* for the people or items to be included;
- the specific kinds of data collection *methods* that will be used;
- the practicalities of *data collection*;
- the processes and techniques for *data analysis*.

The second part of the Methods section tends to be lengthier. It provides an opportunity to explain why the methods are appropriate and to develop an argument that defends the choice of methods on the grounds that they are 'fit for purpose'. This section, therefore, tends to:

- expand on some of the bare bones about the methods;
- evaluate the chosen method and compare this with alternative possibilities;
- use reference to methodology sources in support of the argument.

Access to the necessary sources of data is crucial for the success of a project and the Methods section of the proposal provides an opportunity to describe what measures have been taken in this respect. Authorization that can be obtained in advance will go a long way to allaying any fears the reader might have on this score, and it can prevent the issue of access to necessary data sources becoming a major stumbling block for the proposal.

A discussion of the limitations should be incorporated in any proposal and it is often embedded within the Methods section because it acknowledges the limits to what can, and cannot, be concluded on the basis of the particular design, methods, and scope of the research being proposed. A statement of limitations works on the assumption that:

- there is no such thing as 'perfect' research;
- all research operates within constraints of time and money;
- each research strategy and method has its respective strengths and weaknesses;
- good research acknowledges its own limitations.

Further reading

Dawson, C. (2009) *Introduction to Research Methods: A Practical Guide for Anyone Undertaking a Research Project* (4th edn.). Oxford: How To Books (Chapters 2 and 3).

Krathwohl, D.R. and Smith, N.L. (2005) *How to Prepare a Dissertation Proposal: Suggestions for Students in Education and the Social and Behavioral Sciences*. Syracuse, NY: Syracuse University Press (Chapters 5, 7, and 9).

Marshall, C. and Rossman, G. (2011) *Designing Qualitative Research* (5th edn.). Thousand Oaks, CA: Sage (Chapter 4).

Punch, K. (2006) *Developing Effective Research Proposals* (2nd edn.). Thousand Oaks, CA: Sage (Chapter 5).

Walliman, N. (2005) *Your Research Project: A Step-by-Step Guide for the First-time Researcher*. London: Sage (Chapter 7).

8

PLANNING AND RESOURCES

How long will it take and what will it cost?

• *Planning the time* • *The scale of the project* • *Accounting for the costs* • *Researcher skills* • *Summary of key points* • *Further reading*

Research is never free. It always consumes resources. It always takes time and it costs money. Those who evaluate research proposals will be fully aware of this point and will want to be persuaded that the research can be completed on time with the resources available. They will want to feel assured about the feasibility of the research proposal and will ask themselves:

- Is the research project viable bearing in mind the amount of time, money, and other resources needed for its completion?
- Can the overall project be completed within the time available? Will it meet the deadline?

To provide the readers with satisfactory answers to such questions, good research proposals should include relevant information about the planning and resourcing of the project.

Planning the time

Hours per week

There are only so many hours in a week that any researcher can devote to a piece of research and one thing readers will look for in a proposal, therefore, is some indication of the number of working hours that will be regularly spent on the research. Statements such as the following will provide the kind of information that will prove helpful in trying to judge whether the task is 'do-able' or not within the amount of time available:

Research will be conducted on a full-time basis with a minimum of 40 hours a week spent on the project. (e.g. a full-time PhD student)

During the first two months of the research an average of 6 hours a week will be spent on the research, rising to an average of 30 hours a week in the last two months. (e.g. a full-time master's student doing a dissertation)

An average of 8 hours a week will be allocated to the research. (e.g. a part-time student doing a bachelor's degree project)

Evaluators will appreciate such statements not just for the factual information they contain but also because they send the right signals: they indicate that the researcher has *thought* about the level of commitment that will be necessary and built this into their planning for the research.

Time span for the research

Research projects generally work to a deadline. This limits the time span within which the research must be completed and imposes an explicit time constraint on the research. The time frame for undertaking the project, therefore, should be stated clearly within the research proposal. Information should be provided about when the research is due to commence and when the project will be completed.

What happens between the beginning and the end of the project also deserves attention within the proposal. Readers will appreciate a planned schedule for the research that gives some idea of the main research activities that will be carried out and the sequence in which they are planned. This often takes the form of a Gantt chart (see Figure 8.1), which provides a picture of which activities will be undertaken at which stage.

Such things provide some important information that evaluators need to make a judgement about whether the proposed research can be completed on time. And, just as with the information about the number of hours a week to be devoted to the research, it sends a positive message about the extent of preparation that has gone into the proposed research.

Top tip

Research must be finished on time. If the research is delivered late, it can lose its value or even become worthless.

The scale of the project

Whether the task is do-able within the time that is available will depend on the size of the task and this, in turn, will depend on the amount of data that needs to be collected. Bearing this in mind, the scale of the project should be tailored to meet the resource constraints that exist with respect to the particular kind of project. This point is often overlooked by newcomers to research who believe that their proposal will be deemed worthless unless they set their sights high and promise to deliver something that is very impressive – something like a new theory of economic behaviour, perhaps, or the solution to some major problem such as how to prevent drug addiction. Such aims might be laudable, but achieving them would be more likely to lead to a Nobel Prize than a degree. In the context of a normal research proposal, such things are simply not possible. The resources will not be available and, in any case, if the best brains in the world have not yet managed to achieve these things, why would it be reasonable to assume that a relative newcomer to the field

FIGURE 8.1 Time planning and scheduling for research

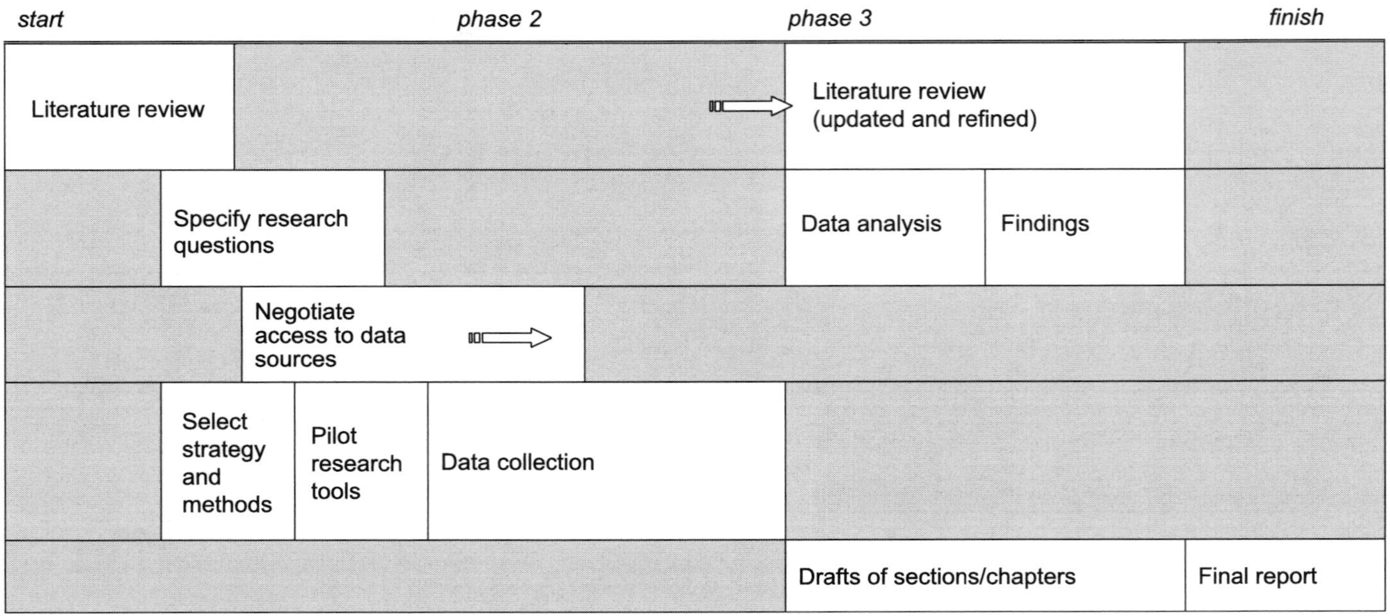

Note: This scheduling does not depict the *volume* of work associated with the research; it deals with the *sequencing* of the work. [from M. Denscombe (2010) *Ground Rules for Social Research*. Maidenhead: Open University Press. p.44)]

could achieve this as part of a bachelor's project, master's dissertation or PhD thesis?

Link up with **Available resources**, p. 21

Top tip
Be realistic about what you can achieve.

In practice, research involves a *compromise* between the information it would be desirable to have and the resources that are available to the researcher. The fact is that research does not take place in an ideal world where time and money are unlimited. In the real world, the chances are that research will need to be curtailed simply because there is neither the time nor the money to carry on beyond a certain point. To illustrate this point, consider the following example:

> My car won't start. Its battery is dead. I wish to conduct some research to find the best replacement battery at the cheapest price. I use an Internet search engine to trawl for information on quality and pricing. Now the quest for the 'best deal' could go on and on but all the time the research is continuing the car is out of action – not working. If I need to get the car going again, then I'll need to stop my research at some point. The more urgently I need the car, the less thorough my research must be. I might need to abandon any idea of finding out which is 'the best deal' available and settle for 'a reasonable deal' based on a quick search – one that will allow me to buy a battery that is 'good enough' and get my car going again. In this case, my research is constrained by a deadline for the findings – I need to buy a battery today, not next week.

In this example, the limits imposed by the deadline for delivery of findings mean that the scale of the research needs to be limited to what can be done within one day and the scope of the research needs to be limited to finding a 'good enough' deal rather than the 'best deal'.

Link up with **Scope and scale of research aims**, p. 50

> **Top tip**
> Rather than propose some perfect research project, the aim should be to propose research that is worthwhile and achievable with the available resources.

Accounting for the costs

The extent to which a proposal is expected to include details about resources varies according to the purpose of the proposal and the scale of the project involved. As a broad rule of thumb, the larger the project the more detail is required about the costs. Where proposals are linked with small projects, and in particular when they are produced in connection with academic degrees, there is generally less need for detailed costings. The reason for this is that larger projects tend to involve substantial sums of money and they often include the work of a number of researchers, factors that inevitably call for the careful monitoring of expenditure and the use of formal accounting procedures. Small-scale projects, on the other hand, tend to use relatively few resources and are more likely to rely on informal, hidden sources of funding for support.

Funding bids

Research proposals that involve bids for large sums of money will need to provide a full and formal breakdown of the costs involved. The proposal will need to list the various items of expenditure, estimate what each will cost, and justify why it is necessary for completion of the project. The purchase of major items will need to have been approved in advance by relevant finance departments. A figure for the costs of 'overheads' to cover the costs of general items such as office accommodation and materials, computing services, telephone calls and so on will need to have been calculated and agreed on the basis of some formula – for instance, a percentage of the total staffing budget for the project.

Where teams of researchers are involved there needs to be information about *the division of labour* within the team and the proportion of hours that each team member will contribute to the project. Research teams will be led by a 'principal investigator' – often referred to just as the 'PI' – and the proposal will need to provide details about:

- the responsibilities of each member (what duties they will have and what expertise they will bring to the project);

- the amount of time each member will devote to the project (e.g. hours per week);
- the costs of 'employing' the team members.

The term 'employing' is in inverted commas because membership of a research team does not always involve the need to create a brand new contract of employment. The team members, along with the principal investigator, might well be employed by a university or research institute and the costs incurred by having these people work as part of the team will be the cost of buying out their time from their existing work contract. Things can get pretty complicated here. There are rules that funding bodies and employing institutions use, and there are accounting practices that all need to be taken into consideration. The underlying point, though, is that researchers' time costs money and the bid for funding will need a calculation of exactly what that cost will be.

It is not surprising, then, that when the research involves teams of people and many thousands of pounds that close attention will be given to formally accounting for the expenditure. The size and complexity of the endeavour require that due care and attention be given to monitoring the budget. When the research requires the purchase of expensive items, the renting of equipment, the use of premises and the efforts of more than one researcher then contracts need to be drawn up and lawyers and accountants become involved. As a consequence, funding organizations invariably insist that applications must be submitted using a form that they supply which requires the costs to be broken down into very specific components.

Projects, dissertations, and theses

In the case of small-scale projects, particularly those undertaken as part of a degree programme at bachelor's, master's or doctoral level, the cost factor does not feature very prominently in a research proposal. There are three main reasons for this.

First, such research makes use of *institutional resources*. When researchers conduct a piece of research while studying at a university or working within an organization they generally rely on a number of resources that can slip under the radar when it comes to thinking about the costs of research. These 'overheads' are not normally brought into the equation but . . . what about the use of an office and the furniture within it, the use of a computer and the software needed for the research, the paper clips, the stapler, the Post-It® notes, and all those other minor incidental things that are used routinely while doing the research – things without which it would impossible to function effectively? Even in the case of proposals in the disciplines of science, technology, engineering, and medicine, which often involve the use of expensive equipment and valuable laboratory time, these vital resources tend to be supplied without needing to be applied for, and approved, as part of the student's research proposal itself. It is generally assumed that the cost of such facilities, services, and equipment is borne by the university (or covered by student fees).

Second, individual researchers tend to *absorb costs* and do not factor in the real costs to themselves when carrying out the research. In small-scale research such as that done as part of a degree, there is an implicit assumption that the project will be carried out on an individual basis and that the research work does not involve delegating work to other people or employing other people or agencies to do the work. A consequence of this is that the researcher will often make use of 'personal' resources to subsidize the research. For example, phone calls might be made from home or text messages sent from a mobile. The home computer might well be used for sending emails and conducting literature searches online. During the evenings and weekends, work on the project is likely to enjoy the comforts of heating and lighting provided at home. The journey to a local research site that only takes half an hour will not drain the petrol tank, and will not be given a second thought. These are just some of the typical ways in which research appears to get done for nothing when, in fact, it relies on a range of vital resources that are not counted (i.e. costs informally absorbed by the researcher).

Perhaps the most significant cost that is absorbed by individual researchers working on small-scale projects is their own time. Research takes time and effort on the part of the researcher and the notion of *opportunity cost* draws attention to the question of what the researcher would have been doing if not spending time on the project. What activities, what pleasures, what rewards does the researcher need to forfeit to undertake the project? Sometimes the opportunity costs 'come with the territory' and are something over which the researcher has little choice. In the context of projects, dissertations, and theses produced for academic degrees, the hours of labour devoted to the research are treated as something that is built into the degree programme; something to be expected as part and parcel of the study that students commit to doing when they enrol on a degree course. For people who conduct research that is not part of a degree programme, however, the opportunity costs might be more visibly a matter of choice. For them, taking the time to conduct the research needs to be seen as a choice that is 'worthwhile', something that is rewarding enough to compensate for the sacrifices that need to be made. The research takes place *instead* of alternative activities – things such as work-related tasks or possibly the leisure activities, family time, and 'me' time that will not happen because the time will be devoted, instead, to the research project.

There are, however, some costs linked with projects, dissertations, and theses that might not be covered by the institution or cannot be absorbed by the researcher. These warrant consideration in advance when thinking about the resources for research. It is definitely a bad idea to start research on a topic only later to realize that there are substantial items of expenditure needed to complete the work. Things to consider include:

- travel costs related to data collection;
- purchase costs for information (e.g. market research reports);
- survey costs (for postal questionnaires);
- specialist computer software for data analysis;
- conference fees (along with travel and accommodation);
- transcription or translation services;
- printing costs for producing the final report.

Top tip

Think about the likely costs involved in the research. Match the scale and scope of the research to the resources that will be available.

Travel, in particular, can prove to be a very expensive item. When planning the research it is worth calculating the likely costs of travel and then considering whether there are ways in which the design of the research might be adapted so that travel costs can be reduced. Rather than the topic being pitched at a national level, would a regional or even local level prove to be more manageable in terms of the travel costs and better suited to the resource envelope within which the research is to be conducted? Will topics that involve international comparisons require travel to other countries and, if so, can this be afforded? Are there alternative ways of getting data from other countries that do not require travel (e.g. use of phone, email or Skype)?

Suppose, for example, that the proposed research is to involve a comparison of team leadership in two organizations, one in the UK and one in India. Initially, the feasibility of conducting such research might seem to depend on the availability of resources to travel between the two research sites. Where will the money come from? The proposal should include some words to allay fears on this matter that evaluators might have. The following statements, in differing ways, would both serve that purpose:

The researcher will visit India for personal reasons and will include the fieldwork as part of a family visit planned to coincide with the research project. The travel costs will not, therefore, require special funding.

Research will be based on interviews with team leaders at the two sites. These interviews will be conducted using Skype and there are no specific resource implications involved with this form of data collection.

Top tip

Explain how significant items of expenditure will be resourced.

Researcher skills

The skills of the researcher are a resource, just like time and money. Different research projects require different skills and when considering the feasibility of conducting a piece of research it is important to bear this in mind. At the point of choosing a topic it is important that the researcher asks: 'Do I have the necessary skills to conduct such a piece of research?'

Of course, there is absolutely nothing wrong with wanting to develop new and different skills to undertake a piece of research, but this does provide an added challenge. For one thing, it takes time, and this is a commodity that can be in short supply when it comes to deadlines for completion of a project. Also, it might take a researcher out of his or her comfort zone.

There are a variety of skills that are required for research. Individuals each have their own personal qualities and skills and they bring these with them when it comes to the research. And there is good sense in 'playing to your strengths'. Perhaps the most obvious example would be skills in data analysis. Those who through their previous training are comfortable with quantitative approaches might be more comfortable with a topic that lends itself to this kind of data analysis. And those whose strengths lie with interpretive skills and who are good with interpersonal communication might be advised to conduct research in an area that lends itself to the use of qualitative data.

In a slightly different sense, the necessary skills can also take the form of qualifications and professional skills that can be essential for undertaking the research. These credentials can be vital for gaining access to particular settings and people and for having the kind of insight about the situation that is crucial for the success of the project. So, for example, in order to undertake research on 'energy conservation in new public buildings' the researcher might be expected to have a background in building technology and environmental issues.

Link up with **Appendix 4: Choosing a research topic**

Top tip
Make the most of your personal resources – your skills, your identity, your networks.

Summary of key points

The resource implications of any proposed piece of research are significant because they have a bearing on the feasibility of the study. Successful proposals will persuade the reader that the planned research stands a realistic chance of being achieved, recognizing that readers will not 'buy into' an idea if they feel that the necessary resources are not available. The question that will always be asked by those who evaluate research proposals is, 'Can the research be done properly with the resources that are available?'

It follows from this that research proposals should not be over-ambitious in terms of their aims or the data they plan to collect. Evaluators will understand that research inevitably involves something of a compromise and what they will be looking for is a project whose scale matches the resources that are available to carry it out.

The key resources that readers will have in mind when evaluating a proposal are *time and planning*. Time is a resource that is as vital as money for the successful completion of a research project. A shortage of time will threaten the quality of the end-product, and if the researcher runs out of time the project will fail. The feasibility of the research, therefore depends on:

- the availability of *working hours* for carrying out the research;
- the *time frame* of the research and the need to meet *deadlines* for completion of the project.

Regarding *costs*, proposals linked to projects, dissertations, and theses are not generally expected to include a detailed account of the full costs involved. Normally, it is only necessary to identify exceptional costs (rather than those services, facilities, and materials supplied by the institution or absorbed by the researcher). Such exceptional items (such as large travel expenses) need to be justified and an explanation needs to be provided about how such special costs will be resourced.

Researcher skills are a resource that needs to be factored into the equation. Researchers need to have the necessary skills to conduct the proposed investigation, and evaluators of the proposal will want to find evidence within the proposal that such skills will be available when the project commences. This can involve *technical skills* and qualifications, or it might involve *personal attributes* that can be usefully employed to facilitate the inquiry (personal identity, networks, and contacts).

Bearing all these points in mind, research proposals should include sufficient information about planning and resourcing to allow readers to make informed judgements about whether the research is feasible. This means that proposals should include, at minimum:

- a schedule for completion of the research in the form of a Gantt chart outlining the plan of work;
- an estimate of the total number of researcher hours needed to complete the work (broken down into preparation, data collection, data analysis, and writing up).

And, even in proposals where detailed costings are not required (such as those linked with bachelor's degree projects, master's degree dissertations, and PhD theses), there should be a note of any exceptional items involving significant costs that are foreseeable in connection with data collection and analysis, and how these will be funded.

Further reading

Denicolo, P. and Becker, L. (2012) *Developing Research Proposals (Success in Research)*. London: Sage (Chapters 7 and 8).

Denscombe, M. (2010) *Ground Rules for Social Research* (2nd edn.). Maidenhead: Open University Press (Chapter 3).

Friedland, A.J. and Folt, C.L. (2000) *Writing Successful Science Proposals*. New Haven: Yale University Press (Chapters 10, 11, and 13).

Locke, L.F., Spirduso, W.W. and Silverman, S.J. (2007) *Proposals that Work: A Guide for Planning Dissertations and Grant Proposals* (5th edn.). Thousand Oaks, CA: Sage (Chapters 8 and 9).

9

RESEARCH ETHICS

Is the research socially acceptable?

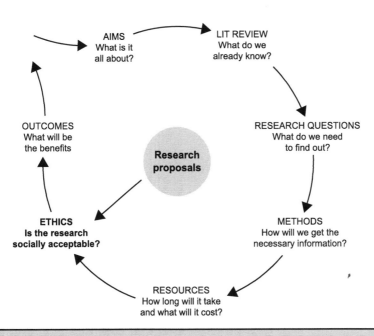

- *What kinds of research need ethical approval? • Do all research proposals need to cover research ethics? • What section of a proposal deals with research ethics? • Codes of research ethics • Principles of research ethics • Risk assessment • Ethics approval • What are evaluators looking for in the proposal? • Summary of key points • Further reading*

When someone embarks on a piece of research there is the possibility that they could end up doing harm rather than good. Research ethics is about setting standards for conducting research that minimize this prospect. A moral stance is taken in relation to research activity which states that research should only be undertaken for good reasons where it is possible to see some beneficial outcome from the project. This means that:

- participants do not suffer harm as a consequence of their involvement in the research;
- the research design and research activity are likely to lead to good quality findings;
- findings contribute to the greater good, and are not used for selfish or malicious purposes.

If a proposal provides any indication that the research might not meet the required standards of ethical behaviour the proposal will be rejected.

What kinds of research need ethical approval?

The types of research that require ethical approval are those that involve:

- Primary data collection *from* human beings and organizations. This includes research using methods such as interviews and questionnaires where people are invited to provide information possibly as part of a survey or a case study.
- Primary data collection *on* human beings and organizations. In this instance people might be involved in a survey that observes their behaviour or an experiment designed to manipulate normal physiological and/or psychological processes.
- Research *about* humans where the individuals involved are *personally identifiable*. This applies to the use of documentary sources and archived data and, even if the research uses data on people who are no longer alive, there might still be ethical issues that need to be considered.

In some disciplines there is an extremely high sensitivity to research ethics; health, medicine, nursing, and genetics top the list. This is not surprising since quite clearly research in these areas can carry obvious risks of causing physical damage to participants. But a concern with the well-being of participants goes beyond protecting them from physical harm. It extends to emotional well-being and to a general concern that those who participate in research should be safeguarded and have their interests protected. And it is worth stressing that this concern is not restricted to just the medical sciences. It is shared by the social sciences, including the disciplines of psychology, sociology, politics and economics, and applied research in areas such as education, business and management, and public policy. The fact is that research ethics are considered highly important for all areas of human research. Those who evaluate research proposals know this and will want to feel reassured that the proposed research meets the necessary ethical standards. And, as Box 9.1 indicates, they will pay particular attention to those kinds of research that they know will need careful handling to maintain appropriate ethical standards.

Box 9.1 Research that requires special care in terms of research ethics

Some kinds of research that would 'normally be considered as involving more than minimal risk':

- Research involving DECEPTION or which is conducted without participants' full and informed consent at the time the study is carried out. [It is, however, recognised that there are occasions when the use of covert research methods is necessary and justifiable.]
- Research involving SENSITIVE TOPICS – for example, participants' sexual behaviour, their illegal or political behaviour, their experience of violence, their abuse or exploitation, their mental health, or their gender or ethnic status.
- Research involving access to records of personal or sensitive CONFIDENTIAL INFORMATION, including genetic or other biological information, concerning identifiable individuals.
- Research which would or might induce PSYCHOLOGICAL STRESS, anxiety or humiliation, or cause more than minimal pain.
- Research involving INTRUSIVE INTERVENTIONS or data collection methods – for example, the administration of substances, vigorous physical exercise, or techniques such as hypnotism.
- Research involving potentially VULNERABLE GROUPS – for example, with children and young people, those with a learning disability or cognitive impairment, or individuals in a dependent or unequal relationship.
- Research involving those who LACK CAPACITY – all research involving those who lack capacity . . . must be approved by an 'appropriate body' operating under the Mental Capacity Act, 2005.
- Research involving groups where PERMISSION OF A GATEKEEPER is normally required for initial access to members, i.e. where access to research participants is not possible without the permission of another person (with appropriate authority).
- Research involving respondents through the INTERNET, in particular where visual images are used, and where sensitive issues are discussed.

- Other research involving visual/vocal methods particularly where participants or other individuals may be IDENTIFIABLE IN THE VISUAL IMAGES used or generated.
- Research undertaken OUTSIDE OF THE UK where there may be issues of local practice and political sensitivities.
- Research where the SAFETY of the researcher may be in question, in particular those working in the field.

Edited from Economic and Social Research Council (2010) *Framework for Research Ethics*. Swindon: ESRC. Available at: http://www.esrc.ac.uk/_images/Framework_for_Research_ Ethics_tcm8-4586.pdf (para. 1.2.3).

Do all research proposals need to cover research ethics?

Some kinds of research might appear to involve no ethical issues. For example, where the research is based on secondary source material, published documents, and information that is already in the public domain, it might be considered that there is no need for any scrutiny of the research ethics involved. This might be true; however, as a general rule, it is good practice to include a section on research ethics whatever the sources of data that are used, and there are two good reasons for this. First, ethical considerations arise not only in relation to the methods of data collection. Even if the data collection itself gives rise to no ethical issues there can still be a range of issues stemming from:

- the subject matter involved;
- the purpose of doing the research;
- how the findings will be used.

Second, and linked with this, readers now *expect* to see research ethics covered in the proposal, even if to the researcher there appear to be no substantial or problematic ethical issues that need to be addressed. Evaluators will feel more assured if they can arrive at that judgement for themselves. And they will also have greater confidence in the proposal if they see that the researcher is conversant with the nature of ethical issues in research and is operating from a position of knowledge rather than ignorance if they claim that there are no ethical issues involved in the proposed piece of research.

> **Top tip**
>
> Research ethics are always relevant. Provide consideration of research ethics in every research proposal.

What section of a proposal deals with research ethics?

Research proposals can consider ethical issues in the Methods section or, preferably, they can provide a separate research ethics section. The benefits of using a separate section are that, as it has just been noted, ethics issues can arise not only in relation to the methods of data collection but also in relation to the topic being studied and the dissemination of findings.

> **Top tip**
>
> Make sure that 'Research ethics' is a clearly visible section within the proposal.

Codes of research ethics

Ideas about what is morally right and what is morally wrong in relation to research are formulated in *codes* of research ethics. These codes are written with specific disciplines and different kinds of practitioners in mind and there are a variety of codes produced by official bodies, research institutions, and professional associations, each written for their own specific community of researchers (see Box 9.2).

> **Box 9.2 Codes of research ethics – some examples**
>
> Association of Business Schools. *Ethics Guide 2010*. Available at: http://www.the-abs.org.uk/files/2010%20Ethics%20Guide%20AGM%20version.pdf
>
> British Educational Research Association. *Ethical Guidelines for Educational Research*. Available at: http://www.bera.ac.uk/files/2011/08/BERA-Ethical-Guidelines-2011.pdf

British Psychological Society. *Ethical Principles for Conducting Research with Human Participants.* Available at: http://www.bps.org.uk/sites/default/files/documents/code_of_ethics_and_conduct.pdf

British Sociological Association. *Statement of Ethical Practice.* Available at: http://http://www.britsoc.co.uk/equality/Statement+Ethical+Practice.htm

Economic and Social Research Council. *The Research Ethics Guidebook: A Resource for Social Scientists.* Available at: http://www.ethicsguidebook.ac.uk/

General Medical Council. *Good Practice in Research.* Available at: http://www.gmc-uk.org/guidance/ethical_guidance/5991.asp

Market Research Society. *MRS Code and Guidelines.* Available at: http://www.marketresearch.org.uk/standards/codeconduct.htm

National Health Service (UK). *National Research Ethics Service.* Available at: http://www.nres.npsa.nhs.uk

Social Research Association. *Ethical Guidelines.* Available at: http://www.the-sra.org.uk/documents/pdfs/ethics03.pdf

UK Government Social Research. Available at: http://www.civilservice.gov.uk/networks/gsr/gsr-code

US Department of Health and Human Services. *Office for Human Research Protections.* Available at: http://www.hhs.gov/ohrp/index.html

There are a number of points about these codes that are worth noting. First, to encourage awareness of the ethical principles these codes are usually made *freely available* online at the relevant websites. Codes of research ethics, therefore, are easily accessible and it is to be expected that writers of a research proposal will be familiar with the relevant code (or codes) for their own research area, discipline background or professional association.

> **Top tip**
> Adhere to a recognized code of research ethics. Identify the most appropriate one for you, and in the proposal show how you have applied this code to your research.

Second, although these codes of research ethics reflect the interests of the particular body they represent they tend to *have a lot in common.* There is a large degree of consistency between the codes – all reflect the basic ethical premises established in the *Nuremberg Code* and the *Declaration of Helsinki.*

A third point to be aware of is that what codes of research ethics actually do is establish *benchmarks* in relation to what is morally acceptable in relation to research activity. The principles for research activity described in the *codes are not a set of hard and fast rules* that can never be broken. This is explicitly recognized by the vast majority of codes. Although some principles will be sacrosanct, the codes acknowledge that with some principles there can be exceptions. In such a case deviation from the principle might be acceptable if it can be explained and defended as necessary and reasonable. For example, the principle might be that researchers should gain 'written consent' from participants; however, the circumstances of a particular piece of research might mean that consent cannot be obtained in a written form. The researcher will need to justify the decision not to obtain consent in writing. This will involve (a) explaining why it is considered necessary to deviate from the principle on this occasion and (b) making the case that the rights and interests of the participants will not be adversely affected in view of the specific nature of the research that is being proposed.

> **Top tip**
> Explain how the research will *apply* ethical principles.

Another reason why codes should not be treated as consisting of hard and fast rules is that ethical issues are not always clear-cut and simple. Complex situations can occur in the real world of research where the *rights and wrongs are not always straightforward*. The benefits of research for a group, for instance, might come with a risk attached and an element of judgement might need to be exercised when deciding if the research will be ethically acceptable. It is in such circumstances that experts on Research Ethics Committees will consider the issues and arrive at a decision to approve the proposed research or not. (See 'Ethics approval' on p. 132.)

There is one other reason that codes do not provide hard and fast rules of conduct. The various codes generally agree that *responsibility for the ethical conduct of research rests ultimately with the individual researcher*. Codes should never be treated as a shield to hide behind. Researchers cannot say 'I followed the rules' or 'I ticked the relevant box' and thereby absolve themselves of personal responsibility for what goes on. They always remain responsible for their own decisions when conducting research.

> **Top tip**
> The ethical conduct of a piece of research is the researcher's personal responsibility.

Principles of research ethics

There are three themes that are evident in all codes of research ethics and, although the codes vary somewhat in terms of their emphasis and the way they formulate the ideas, it is easy to see the legacy of the *Nuremberg Code* and the *Declaration of Helsinki* in all of them.

No harm

First and foremost, research should avoid harm being caused to those who participate in the research. This includes the researchers as well. They should be no worse off as a consequence of their participation. Harm is a broad term and, in this context, this deliberately prompts the researcher to consider all kinds of harm that might occur. Physical harm is the most obvious form, but social research needs to consider as well a range of other ways in which participation (in the particular piece of research being proposed) could adversely affect people. The types of harm to be considered include:

- psychological (e.g. feelings of stress, loss of confidence, experiencing trauma);
- social (e.g. having reputation ruined, losing face, having relationships damaged);
- economic (e.g. losing sources of income, being denied a promotion at work);
- physical (e.g. causing illness, infection or even disability);
- safety (e.g. becoming a victim of an attack or being put in dangerous circumstances);
- legal (e.g. being exposed in terms of benefits fraud or tax evasion);
- equality and justice (e.g. sense of unfairness or losing out relative to others).

Researchers need to take 'all reasonable precautions' to protect the interests of participants and to ensure, as far as is it is reasonably possible to do so, that no-one is directly harmed as a result of their participation in the research project.

> **Top tip**
> Research that harms people is unacceptable.

Voluntary consent

Participation should be completely voluntary and there should be no kind of force, coercion, moral blackmail or any other means of pressuring someone to take part in research against their will. It is legitimate to offer minor inducements to reward people for giving up their time to take part in the research, but it is not acceptable for researchers to bribe people or to exert any undue pressure to 'encourage' their participation.

Consent should be provided by participants, and this consent should be *informed*. There is an obligation on researchers to provide potential participants with a sufficient amount of information about the purposes of the research and the nature of their involvement for them to make a decision (about whether or not to participate) that is 'informed'. They need to know what they are getting themselves into. This is why the notion of 'informed consent' lies at the heart of ethical research.

Getting consent from participants is not the end of the story. There is a clear and explicit understanding in terms of research ethics that this *consent can be withdrawn at any time* – participants have the *right to withdraw* from the research at any stage. If they change their minds they are at liberty to curtail their involvement even though they might have provided written consent at the start. And participants should be made aware of this right.

There are two other things that it is important to bear in mind in relation to the informed consent principle. First, some codes of ethics insist that the consent should be *in writing*, whereas others do not. Different disciplines vary in the emphasis placed on this. Second, *children and vulnerable adults* need to be treated with special care in terms of gaining their consent for involvement in research. Getting consent is not simply a matter of getting people to sign on the dotted line: age and mental capacity need to be taken into consideration.

Scientific integrity

Researchers are expected to approach their work in a way that upholds high professional standards. In the first instance this means ensuring that the research will make use of *suitable methods*. The thinking on this point is that any research which employs methods that are not 'the best available' will inevitably produce findings that are not of the highest quality. At best, this will waste the time of participants and any other stakeholders in the research. At worst, the use of inappropriate or poor methods might cause harm to the participants.

Linked with this, there is an expectation that the *researcher is competent* to conduct the investigation. He or she is expected to be proficient in the use of the methods and techniques involved in the research and to have the appropriate experience and qualifications to carry out the research. The demands of the specific research project, in other words, should not exceed the capabilities of the researcher.

Link up with **Researcher skills**, p. 118

The notion of 'scientific integrity' also carries with it the idea that the researcher should be *open and honest* in all dealings with participants and colleagues connected with the research. For example, this entails:

- being truthful in their dealing with participants. Researchers should avoid any misrepresentation of their work and should not engage in any deception relating to the investigation;
- enabling participants to check the identity and bona fides of the researcher;
- avoiding any plagiarism or similar misuse of other people's work.

Scientific integrity also conveys a notion of objectivity, and in this spirit there is an expectation that researchers should *avoid bias* in their work. To this end, they are expected to:

- declare any sponsorship or vested interests that might be linked to the research and its findings;
- be fair and honest in the treatment of the data;
- operate with a sense of justice and fair play in terms of who gets selected to participate in the research and who gets to reap the benefits – a point stressed by the Belmont Report (1979).

Link up with **The need for an open-minded approach**, p. 86

There is another 'moral' obligation relating to the conduct of research that sits alongside the three core themes of research ethics. That is the requirement for *compliance with the law and technical regulations.* Research activity should always operate within these parameters. Researchers, for example, can be required to ensure *data retention.* Such requirements are mainly enforced in relation to funded research where the aim is to make data available for future reference. The length of time varies depending on the auspices under which the research takes place – it can vary from 3 to 10 years and, in the case of some medical research, a minimum of 20 years.

There are also legal constraints to be considered. There are no exceptions for researchers with regard to the law. No matter how good the intention of the research might be, researchers must not engage in fraud to obtain their data or undertake any other illegal activity in pursuit of their data. If caught, they will get charged and prosecuted just like anybody else would. Ways in which research activity comes face to face with legal requirements include:

- *Ownership of the data and intellectual property*: Researchers need to be careful about establishing ownership rights when it comes to the collection of, and use of, data involving collaboration with other researchers and organizations.

- *Data security*: Researchers need to be aware of the relevant legislation and ensure that data from the research will be stored securely in line with data protection principles. They should also make sure that data are not passed on to third parties who have no connection with the research. The data must only be used for the purposes they were originally collected for.
- *Methods*: Researchers need to be sure that their methods are above board and totally legal. This means taking care not to get involved with research that involves unauthorized access to material (particularly with internet research).
- *Topic*: Researchers, especially newcomers, would do well to steer clear of topics like terrorism, child pornography, etc., for fear that their research activity could cross a fine line dividing legitimate data collection from illegal activity.

Risk assessment

It is good practice for some kind of risk assessment to be undertaken. In the case of projects, dissertations, and theses, this will normally be something conducted informally: student research projects are not normally expected to go through a formal risk assessment procedure. However, in the case of larger funded research projects, there is now a growing tendency to conduct a *formal* risk assessment. This involves having the project looked at by a person or committee who will give detailed consideration to the potential risks associated with conducting a specific piece of research.

In the context of research ethics the primary concern will be the *risk of harm* that might potentially result from the research. Consideration will be given to aspects of the research such as the nature of data collection, the means for keeping data secure, and plans for disseminating findings to determine what likelihood there is, if any, that participants might suffer some harm as a consequence of their involvement in the project. The purpose, then, is to anticipate potential problems and amend the design of the research to build in necessary safeguards to avoid the risks. The key word here is 'potential'. Researchers are expected to take into consideration not only the occurrence of bad things that *will certainly* happen as a consequence of their research but also the harm that *might possibly* happen. This extends the scope of things that warrant consideration and means that researchers need to be very cautious – thinking about a whole range of 'What if . . .?' scenarios in connection with their proposed research.

Link up with **Risk assessment**, p. 103

Ethics approval

Research activity will almost certainly need to go through a process of 'ethics approval' before it is allowed to go ahead. Sometimes this approval will be based on information contained *within* a research proposal. The section of the proposal devoted to research ethics will cover the necessary issues. This 'light touch' approach might be the case, for instance, where a proposal is submitted to a university tutor in respect of an undergraduate degree project. More commonly, ethics approval requires the completion of a separate form devised purely for the purpose. Such forms are known as *ethics protocols*. These forms pay detailed attention to the various ethical issues that might arise in relation to the research. They are submitted for approval to *Research Ethics Committees* (also known as Institutional Review Boards in the USA). The process of approval and the demands of the forms are most rigorous in the fields of health and medicine but the use of stand-alone ethics protocols is also widespread in relation to research degrees and funded research in other disciplines as well (see Remenyi et al. 2011).

If for any reason the appropriate research ethics committee does *not* grant ethics approval the project will be halted. It will need to be abandoned or it will need to be revised in a manner that meets the committee's concerns.

Top tip

Research projects will not normally go ahead until they receive ethical approval.

Evaluators of research proposals know this and it gives them a double reason for paying close attention to any ethical issues arising from the proposed research. On a matter of principle they will not wish to support a research proposal that worries them on ethical grounds. And, in a practical sense, they will not wish to give the green light to a proposal if they have any doubts about whether the proposed research will be approved by the relevant research ethics committee. The existence of a parallel ethics approval system, then, does not eliminate the need for research proposals to address the issue of research ethics. On the contrary, it actually reinforces the evaluators' sensitivity to ethics issues and underlines the need for *research ethics to be dealt with as an integral part of any research proposal.*

What are the evaluators looking for in the proposal?

First, readers will want reassurance that the proposed research will go through a process of *ethics approval* before it is allowed to go ahead. All that is required on this point is a simple statement – just one or two sentences – that specifies (a) the committee or other authority to which the application has been made and (b) whether the project is still awaiting approval or approval has already been obtained. Obviously, it is preferable if ethics approval has already been obtained.

Second, a simple statement about which *code of research ethics* will be adhered to during the project will pay dividends. All that is needed is a few words that name the code, give its web address, and state that the researcher is committed to undertaking the research in accord with the principles contained in that code. The code, of course, needs to be the most relevant bearing in mind the qualifications of the researcher and the topic of the research.

Third, some brief demonstration that the researcher is aware of the *core principles* of research ethics can be valuable. Simply citing a code of research ethics will not be enough, on its own, to convince the reader that the researcher is aware of the principles and issues that need to be addressed. And so a brief comment that reveals some knowledge about the core principles and key issues can prove useful. This should *not* entail a list of the principles. It should simply consist of a couple of sentences that identify the three core principles and acknowledge the fundamental need of all research to respect these principles. The statement could take the following form:

> The research will abide by the principles contained in the [named] code of research ethics. The research will ensure (as far as is possible) that no harm is done to participants, that participation is voluntary, and that the research will be conducted with appropriate standards of scientific/ professional integrity.

Application of the principles

Having made a commitment to the core principles of research ethics the research proposal should then proceed to spell out exactly how those principles will be put into action – how they will be *applied*. Providing a list of the principles of research ethics will not suffice. Evaluators want to know how these will be put into practice. They will want to know *how* the interests of participants will be protected and *how* the matter of research integrity will be addressed.

On the matter of potential *harm to participants*, readers will want to see answers to questions such as:

- What kinds of harm are reasonably foreseeable? What precautions will be taken to prevent these occurring? Are there any safety issues? How will these be overcome?

- If the research involves young people or vulnerable groups, what special measures will be implemented?
- Has authorization been obtained for access to potential participants? Is a Criminal Records Bureau (CRB) check required and, if so, has it been obtained?
- What measures will be taken to guarantee the anonymity of participants? Will anonymity be guaranteed in terms of any reported findings from the research?
- What assurances about confidentiality will be given? How will data security be safeguarded? Who will have access to the data files? What assurances can be given about non-disclosure of information to third parties?
- Will the research avoid undue intrusion into personal lives? Will it respect participants' rights to privacy?
- Are there any aspects of the proposed research that might entail a threat to the interests of participants? Have these been described and have they been defended bearing in mind the extent of the potential harm involved?

Top tip

Describe what measures will be taken to protect the interests of the participants.

On the matter of *voluntary participation and informed consent* readers will want answers to things such as:

- How will consent be obtained? What kind of consent will be required? Will a consent form be used? How will this be administered?
- Will the research require *written* consent or not?
- When and where will potential participants be provided with a 'participant's information document'?
- Will potential participants be formally notified of their right to withdraw?
- Are there any considerations about equality, fairness, and justice that arise in connection with the selection of participants for the research?
- Does the research rely on any form of deception? Has this deception been justified (for instance, as essential for the viability of the research)?

On the matter of *scientific integrity*, readers will want answers to questions such as:

- What research experience and technical skill does the researcher have, and is this suitable for the nature of the research envisaged in the proposal?

- What measures will be in place to support impartiality? Is there a statement from the researcher about any vested interests in the findings or any other conflict of interest?
- How will open dealings with participants and colleagues be encouraged? What avenues of communication will be open between researcher and participants? How will participants be able to check the credentials of the researcher?
- Are there any matters relating to intellectual property or ownership of the data that are likely to arise and, if so, how will these be dealt with?
- Are there any aspects of the research that involve potential bias? Has the source of this bias been explained and its repercussions been openly discussed in the proposal?

Summary of key points

All proposals should include a statement about research ethics so that those who evaluate the proposals can feel confident that the work will meet appropriate ethical standards. There should be a section that identifies any ethical issues that could arise and outlines how those issues will be dealt with. This applies to proposals involving all kinds of human research. It is good practice to undertake a *risk assessment* with regard to any potential harm arising from the research.

Ethics approval is normally required before any research project is allowed to go ahead. The process of ethics approval often works in parallel with the process for approving the proposed research.

The standards that need to be met are outlined in *codes of research ethics*. Such codes provide benchmarks for what is morally acceptable in relation to research activity. Researchers should be familiar with the code of research ethics for their own research area, discipline background or professional association. Within the proposal the researcher needs to identify with, and commit to, a named code of research ethics. The key principles of research ethics contained in the codes cover three broad areas:

- No harm to participants
- Voluntary consent
- Scientific integrity.

The responsibility for conducting research in an ethical manner always rests with the individual. Codes of research ethics provide guidelines that individual researchers can use to assure themselves that the design and conduct of their research meet appropriate standards.

Any research activity that does not comply with the core principles needs to be explicitly *justified* in the proposal. Such exceptions tend to revolve around things like (a) gaining written consent or (b) the use of deception. To be clear, though, ethics committees will *not* condone exceptions if those involve the use of illegal activity or harm to participants. These principles are sacrosanct.

The success of a proposal depends on describing how ethical principles will be *applied*. The proposal needs to specify *what measures and what precautions* will be taken to make sure that the principles will be upheld. The proposal needs to explain how the research will deal with matters such as:

- *Preventing harm*: through specifying the safeguards employed for those being researched.
- *Respecting privacy*: through showing how the research respects personal rights (e.g. avoid undue intrusion into personal lives).
- *Protecting identities*: through outlining the measures used (e.g. guarantees of anonymity in any reported findings from the research).
- *Gaining consent*: through describing procedures for getting informed agreement (e.g. use of information sheets, consent forms).
- *Respecting confidentiality*: through noting restrictions around the disclosure of information (e.g. data protection, data security).
- *Ensuring impartiality*: through highlighting any means of avoiding bias in the research (e.g. by declaring any vested interests in findings).
- *Being honest and open*: through the avoidance of deception or misrepresentation (e.g. online availability of details about the researcher and his or her institution).
- *Upholding research integrity*: through using good quality design and suitable methods (e.g. reference to researcher credentials and experience).

Further reading

Economic and Social Research Council (undated) *The Research Ethics Guide Book: A Resource for Social Scientists*. Available at: http://www.ethicsguidebook.ac.uk.

Israel, M. and Hay, I. (2006) *Research Ethics for Social Scientists: Between Ethical Conduct and Regulatory Compliance*. London: Sage (Chapters 3, 5–7).

Oliver, P. (2010) *The Student's Guide to Research Ethics* (2nd edn.). Maidenhead: Open University Press (Chapters 1, 2, and 9).

Remenyi, D., Swan, N. and Van Den Assem, B. (2011) *Ethics Protocols and Research Ethics Committees*. Reading: Academic Publishing International (Chapters 1, 4, and 8).

10

RESEARCH OUTCOMES

What will be the benefits?

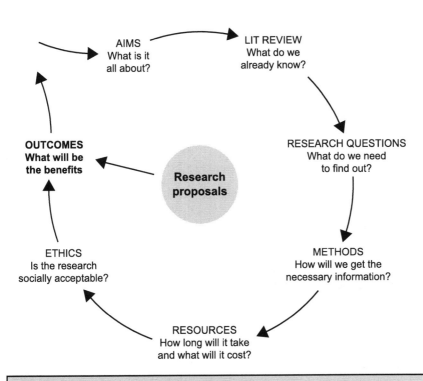

- Value for money • Outcomes and findings • Types of outcomes
- Dissemination of findings • Impact • Summary of key points
- Further reading

Good research is undertaken for a purpose. It is not done out of idle curiosity or done for self-amusement. It is undertaken for a good reason with something beneficial resulting from the time and effort that will go into the project. That is why those who evaluate research proposals will look for information about the *outcomes* from the research. They will want to know about the 'deliverables' that will be produced by the research.

Value for money

All research takes time and effort on the part of the researcher, many projects require the cooperation of participants, and some projects incur significant costs in terms of things like travel and equipment. Research never comes 'for free'. Bearing this in mind, those who evaluate proposals will want to be persuaded that the research will be worthwhile when they weigh up the resources put into the investigation against the eventual benefits that might emerge from the project. They will ask, 'Is it worth it?'

This line of thinking will be most explicit where proposals are produced to compete for research funding. On these occasions there will be a literal sense in which the evaluators will judge the proposals in terms of what they can deliver relative to the price that needs to be paid. With limited money available to fund many applications, the question will inevitably arise about which among the proposals offers the best value for money.

The same mindset, however, will operate with other kinds of research proposals. The evaluators of the proposal will want to know what the benefits of the work will be and they will look to the Outcomes section to help them decide if the research really represents good value for money.

Top tip

Imagine that someone who has read your proposal turns to you and says 'So what?' The Outcomes section should contain your retort. It should identify the kinds of things that will be produced by the research – things that will be of evident value.

Outcomes and findings

A vital distinction needs to be made between 'outcomes' and 'findings'. Outcomes can be stated ahead of the actual research, whereas findings cannot.

A proposal must never suggest that the research will result in particular *findings*. To do so, the researcher would have to know the findings in advance of carrying out the research and there are only two ways they could do this: (a) fabricate the results or (b) conduct the research in a way that is not open to findings that contradict the researcher's prior assumptions. Neither option is permissible if the research is to have any scientific integrity or meet ethical standards for research. Researchers can have hunches about what the findings might be. They can produce hypotheses that state what findings might be expected. But the point of any research is to test these and to approach things with an open mind, thus entertaining the possibility of being proved wrong.

Outcomes are a different thing. Whereas findings are concerned with the results and the specifics of what the data might reveal, outcomes are concerned with the *use* to which these findings are put. Outcomes are about how the findings will be applied and how they will be made available. And this *is* something that can be included at the planning stage before the research begins.

> **Top tip**
> Outcomes are not the same as findings. Be careful not to confuse the two.

Types of outcomes

There is no definitive list of outcomes that are good and acceptable. Outcomes can take a variety of forms and the type of outcome envisaged in a proposal will reflect to a large extent the particular kind of research involved. Some research will lead to outcomes that are of relevance to developments in theory, whereas others like applied research will be more likely to produce practical outcomes. There are, however, some fairly common types of outcomes that are to be found in good research proposals and, for the purposes of making clear the kind of things that constitute outcomes, some of these are listed below. The research can:

Supply *new information*. The research might be designed to move things forward by filling in a gap in what is known on a particular topic. From the start we might know the kind of information that is required, but the precise information can only be discovered through the process of research itself. What can be said at the proposal stage, however, is that a particular gap exists and that the anticipated outcome of the project is to supply that information.

Make *recommendations* relating to a problem. For research geared to practical problems one of the main outcomes from the project might be a series of recommendations aimed at solving the problem or preventing its occurrence in the future. Before the research starts it may not be possible to say exactly what those recommendations will be, but it is still quite reasonable to see the production of a set of recommendations as a tangible end-product – something hopefully of value, and something that will make a difference.

Produce *guidelines* for good practice. Rather than focus on resolutions to specific problems, as recommendations might do, the research might seek to produce more general guidelines that can be applied across a broader range of situations. The design of the research would, of course, need to enable these more generalized suggestions for new practices to emerge from the research but, provided this is the case, guidelines for good practice constitute a solid, tangible output from the project that can be stated in the proposal.

Write a *report* or make a presentation. Research can culminate in the writing of a report or the delivery of the findings verbally in a formal presentation to the 'client group' for the research. The term 'client' in this context can be used quite loosely and does not necessarily mean that they have literally sponsored or paid for the research. This may be the case, but the presentation could equally be provided for any of the stakeholders in the research process. So, for example, research conducted on the use of computers in school could have 'a presentation of findings to staff in the school' as an outcome. Or, a brief report summarizing the findings would serve a similar purpose. Either way, it offers a delivered outcome from the research.

Provide an *insight* that helps to clarify a current debate or controversy. Research that engages with debates or controversies in a field of study can treat the new insight as a distinct outcome from the research. Here, the point of the research is to delve into the issues and use the research project to produce new angles and new ideas that can enhance the quality of the debate and help to move things forward. As an outcome, however, this can appear to be rather vague and nebulous, lacking definite substance. *Publishing* the contribution to the debate, in whatever format, makes the outcome far more tangible and if this is a realistic possibility it is wise to make it an integral part of the outcome. How far this is possible, of course, will depend on the nature of the proposal and whether it is part of a bachelor's project, master's dissertation, PhD application or bid for research funding.

Make a contribution to the *development of a theory* or concept. A research project can be designed to make a contribution to a theory or concept or it can work towards refining a definition of some phenomenon. The contribution will operate at a more abstract level, dealing with analyses, conceptualizations, philosophies, ideas, and ways of thinking about particular things. In a similar vein to insights into a debate or controversy this can provide enormous benefit as an outcome if the researcher is able to commit to putting the contributions into a published format, although the same caveat operates with regard to the level of the work and the fact that proposals such as those for bachelor's projects or master's dissertation might not be expected to produce such outcomes in published form bearing in mind the researcher's limited experience and the time constraints involved.

> **Top tip**
>
> Make outcomes 'tangible'. State how they will be delivered – in what format, for what end (e.g. a project report, a dissertation or thesis, a published paper, a seminar presentation).

Dissemination of findings

The outcomes from a piece of research, if they are to prove to be of real value, need to be communicated and made available to a wider audience. This is the thinking that has taken increasing prominence in recent years in relation to PhD research and funded research. In these cases, a growing emphasis is being placed on the need not only to obtain good and worthwhile findings but also to ensure that those findings reach as wide an audience as possible. What use and what value have findings if no-one gets to hear about them?

Plans for publicizing the findings and for the dissemination of results are, therefore, important for the research in general and the outcomes from the research in particular. Evaluators of the proposal will look to see what strategy there is for the dissemination of findings and publicizing the results. The use of websites is extremely valuable in this respect (Denscombe 2005). A *research website* can be used to disseminate findings to all those who have an interest in the project in a way that is easily accessible, quickly updated, and relatively inexpensive to maintain.

In the case of funded research the expectations are likely to be higher. At this level the outcomes from research can involve the delivery of papers at academic conferences, the publication of findings in peer-reviewed journals, and exposure of the findings in the media through interviews on TV or the radio, or through coverage of the project in the national press. These are not expectations that are held for research conducted for academic awards at bachelor's, master's or PhD level, but they do illustrate the importance of communication for successful research.

> **Top tip**
>
> When disseminating findings take care to maintain the confidentiality of the data and protect the anonymity of participants.

Link up with **Chapter 9: Research Ethics**
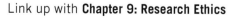

Impact

The wider the dissemination of the findings the more impact the research is likely to have. If no-one knows about the findings other than the student and his or her supervisor then they are unlikely to have any impact. If the results are globally distributed, on the other hand, the research is more likely to influence the thinking of other researchers, the activities of practitioners, and the policies espoused by politicians. An impact on thinking, action, and policies is regarded as a key criterion of good research by the evaluators of research today, and so the outcomes from the research as presented in the proposal should indicate where possible the ways in which the project is likely to have an effect on relevant people.

The value of research is often gauged in terms of notions like 'stakeholder engagement', 'user group involvement', and 'community participation'. These notions, each in their own way, point to the importance that is attributed today to outcomes from research whose influence goes beyond scholarly circles and academic debate to touch the lives of those who are affected by, or have an interest in, the research and its findings. The emphasis is clearly on the usefulness of the research and the applicability of its findings, and the anticipated outcomes from the research are expected, more and more, to show:

- which groups will be affected by the research;
- how they will become engaged with the project;
- what the benefits for them are likely to be.

> **Top tip**
> Emphasize the potential usefulness of the findings.

Summary of key points

Proposals need to state clearly what outcomes are envisaged from the research. These outcomes need to be specified because they play a particularly important role in relation to the task of distinguishing excellent proposals from the rest. Funding bodies and others who evaluate proposals look to the anticipated outcomes as a crucial factor when deciding the relative worth of the proposed research. They will want to know what the research will produce and what it will deliver.

Outcomes should not be confused with findings. Outcomes refer to what will be *done* with the findings from research and this is something that it is possible to predict in advance of doing the research. End-products to research can take the form of:

- practical guidelines and recommendations;
- theoretical contributions to debates and concepts.

In either case, the outcomes become more 'tangible' when they are manifested in some form of publication or event. Plans for the *dissemination* of findings should be stated in the proposal – particularly in the case of funding applications and PhD research proposals. Research websites are particularly valuable in this respect.

Finally, the potential *impact* of the research can have a bearing on whether the research is considered to be worthwhile and this, of course, affects the prospects of the proposal's success. Therefore, the proposal should provide information on the usefulness of the outcomes from the research and which groups might benefit from the research. It should consider how receptive particular groups are likely to be and how eager they might be to respond to the new findings. In a nutshell, it should highlight *who will be interested in the findings and how they will be affected.*

Further reading

Economic and Social Research Council (undated) *Impact Assessment.* Swindon: ESRC. Available at: http://www.esrc.ac.uk/impacts-and-findings/impact-assessment/.

Gerrish, K. and Lacey, A. (2010) *The Research Process in Nursing* (6th edn.). Chichester: Wiley-Blackwell (Chapter 37).

Hughes, C. (ed.) (2003) *Disseminating Qualitative Research in Educational Settings: A Critical Introduction.* Maidenhead: Open University Press

Research Councils UK (undated) *Research Outcomes System.* Swindon: RCUK. Available at: http://www.rcuk.ac.uk/research/Pages/ResearchOutcomesProject.aspx.

Appendix 1

CHECKLIST FOR THE SUBMISSION OF A RESEARCH PROPOSAL

Prior considerations

You should be able to answer 'yes' to these questions

1. Are you sending the proposal to the *right place*? Have you targeted the right organization or individual? Does it meet the requirements of the organization or people who will assess it?
2. Can you *meet the deadline* for submitting the proposal? Will you be able to produce the proposal in time?
3. Have you the *competence and skills* to tackle the topic? Do you have the necessary qualifications or experience?
4. Will you be able to get *access to the data*? Have you sought permission from relevant people or organizations to authorize the research? Are there significant costs for access to vital information?
5. Have you done a *risk assessment* in relation to factors that might hinder the completion of the project?

	You should be able to answer 'yes' to these questions

The proposal itself

6. Does the proposal provide a succinct, precise, clearly written account of the proposed investigation? Does it
   - describe *what* will be done?
   - justify *why* it should be done?
   - indicate *how* it will be done?
7. Have you highlighted the potential *benefits* of the proposed investigation (its value, its outcomes, its contribution, its impact)?
8. Has emphasis been placed on what is *new* or original about the proposed research?
9. Has the topic been linked to *relevant research findings*, theoretical issues, conceptual developments, and practical concerns in the field of study (review of literature, sources cited, up-to-date material)?
10. Have clear and specific *research questions* been identified?
11. Is the *research design* coherent and does the proposal show how the data and the analysis suit the purpose of the particular investigation?
12. Does the proposal acknowledge any *limitations* relating to the research and the kind of conclusions that can be drawn from its findings?
13. Has a plan been presented showing how the research can be completed within the allotted *time frame*?
14. Have the *costs* of investigation (e.g. travel, materials, data) been estimated and do these accord with the amount of resources available for the research?
15. Does the proposal reassure readers that the research is *feasible* (access to data, time, costs)?
16. Within the proposal, is there an explicit consideration of potential *ethical and legal issues* arising from the research?
17. Will the proposal convince the reader that you have *ability and experience* to undertake the research successfully?
18. Is it evident in the proposal that a *risk* assessment has taken place?
19. Has care been taken to *avoid any plagiarism* within the proposal?

Appendix 2

SPECIMEN RESEARCH PROPOSAL

Research Proposal

Smoking Cessation among Young People:
A study of the attitudes and experiences of 15–16-year-olds in relation to the decision to quit smoking

Name: Alex Baker

Submitted to: Department of Social Sciences, Redforest University

Date: June 20xx

Word count: 2095

Table of Contents   Page

1. Title 1

2. Keywords 1

3. Aims 1

4. Background 2

5. Literature review 2

6. Research Questions 3

7. Research Methods 4

8. Planning and Resources 7

9. Research ethics 8

10. Research Outcomes 9

11. References 10

1. Title
Smoking Cessation Among Young People:
A study of the attitudes and experiences of 15–16-year-olds in relation to the decision to quit smoking.

2. Keywords
Smoking cessation; young people; health-related behaviour; tobacco use; cigarettes.

3. Aims
To help reduce the prevalence of tobacco smoking, especially among young people.

To provide knowledge that will improve health education and health promotion targeted at young smokers.

To contribute to existing evidence on the extent to which young smokers attempt to quit smoking by the age of 15–16 years.

To understand the attitudes and experiences of young people who engage in efforts to quit smoking.

To identify the factors perceived by young people to be significant for the success or failure of their attempts to quit smoking.

> **Comment:** The aims start wide and become progressively more specific.

4. Background
Cigarette smoking is the single most preventable cause of premature death in the developed world (WHO 2006). Throughout the world it is estimated that five million people die each year as a result of smoking tobacco and that, on the basis of current trends, this figure is set to rise to 10 million a year by 2030 (WHO 2006).

> **Comment:** Instantly captures the attention of the reader and indicates that the research will tackle an important and worthwhile matter.

Health education campaigns and health promotion measures have helped to reduce the prevalence of cigarette smoking. In England, for instance, there has been a substantial fall in the proportion of adults who smoke cigarettes, down from 39% in 1980 to 21% in 2008. However, worrying levels of smoking persist – especially among young people (ASH 2011). Although there has been a decline in the number of young people who smoke cigarettes there remains a significant minority who are regular smokers. Official figures for England indicate that 12% of 15-year-olds smoke at least once a week (Fuller 2011). This is of particular concern

> **Comment:** Narrows the focus from a global issue to something that is more specific and which can be tackled by the research. Also spells out the need for the research.

because young people are the smokers of the future. As Denscombe (2010: 426) points out, 'they are the most significant group of potential recruits to the ranks of smokers and, as early starters, they are likely to suffer the accumulated effects of smoking over a longer period of their lifetime'.

5. Literature review

The vast majority of initiatives to tackle the problem of smoking among 'under-age' smokers are based on efforts to deter young people from experimenting with tobacco use and reducing the likelihood of them starting to smoke in the first place (Grimshaw and Stanton 2010). Very little attention has been paid to the circumstances surrounding the self-initiated cessation of smoking by young people.

> **Comment:** This establishes the need for the specific research that is being proposed.

There is, however, some evidence that many of those who start smoking at a young age would, by the time they reach 15–16 years, wish to quit smoking. In many cases they have tried to do so, albeit unsuccessfully (Dozois et al. 1995; Stanton et al. 1996b). But there is also evidence that some successfully quit smoking by the time they reach the age of 15–16 years (Centers for Disease Control and Prevention 2009). Denscombe and Drucquer (1999) found that one in eight young people reported having given up a smoking habit by the age of 15–16 years and Stanton et al. (1996a) found a similar proportion in their survey of 15-year-olds.

> **Comment:** Previous findings support the idea behind the proposed research.

In view of the importance for future health of reducing the prevalence of smoking among school-aged children there is a need for more knowledge and insight about the young people who try to quit smoking and, in particular, those who actually manage to quit smoking of their own volition. The investigation will develop and apply existing research evidence based on *adult* smokers which indicates that smoking cessation tends to be a process involving multiple efforts and many failed attempts (DiClemente et al. 1991; Sutton 1994; Clark et al. 1998).

> **Comment:** This identifies the theoretical position underlying the approach to the research.

The proposed research will first seek to check the small number of previous research findings that indicate that a small proportion of 'under-age' smokers want to quit smoking and, in some cases, have become ex-smokers by the age of 15–16 years. It will then try to establish why young people under the age of 16 might want to give up smoking. Focusing on those young people who have tried to quit smoking already, the research will look at their feelings and experiences during the process of trying to quit.

> **Comment:** This links the literature review to the research questions that follow.

Understanding the motives and experiences of those young people seeking to quit smoking can provide valuable new knowledge that draws on real-world experiences of those who have tried and those who have been successful in their efforts. Such young people provide a potentially rich source of data in relation to theories about the social and psychological circumstances surrounding decisions to quit smoking. On the basis of the findings it will be possible to produce recommendations and guidelines for the production of health education materials and health promotion campaigns targeted at smoking cessation among young smokers.

> **Comment:** Here is the USP – something that this research offers that has not been done before. Potentially there will be new knowledge and practical outcomes from the research, reinforcing the case that the research will be worthwhile.

6. Research questions

- What proportion of young people perceive themselves as having given up smoking by the age of 16 years?
- What proportion of young smokers would like to quit smoking if they could, and what proportion have attempted to do so?
- How persistent are young people who smoke in their efforts to quit smoking?
- What do young people regard as powerful motives for giving up smoking?
- What are the experiences and feelings that accompany young people's attempts to quit smoking?
- In what ways do family, friends, and health services support or inhibit young people's efforts to quit smoking?

> **Comment:** The six research questions involve specific things that will be looked at in order to address the aims of the research.

7. Methods

Data collection

The research will use a mixed methods strategy. It will combine quantitative data from a questionnaire survey with qualitative data gathered from focus groups and a photographic diary. Initially, the research will use a questionnaire survey of young people aged 15–16 years ($n = 1800$). The survey will use a cluster sampling technique based on 12 schools in a central region of England. On known attributes of the local population and education authorities, these schools will be selected to be representative in terms of their pupil composition (social class, ethnic composition, urban/suburban/rural location). A web-based questionnaire will be used, with pupils completing the questionnaire during school time. The questionnaire survey will provide baseline data on the prevalence of 'quitting', on the social background of those involved, and on relevant dispositional indicators related to smoking and health-risking behaviour.

Data from the survey will provide stimulus material for a series of *focus groups* that will be conducted with a purposive sample of the 15–16-year-olds ($n = 48$). Two focus groups will be conducted in a sub-sample of four of the collaborating schools. The first focus group will comprise six young people who have quit smoking. A second focus group with will comprise six young smokers who have not quit, acting as a comparative control group.

Photo-elicitation techniques will be used as a means for probing the personal experiences of 15–16-year-olds who are actively trying to quit smoking. Two such pupils from the sub-sample of the four schools will be invited to construct a *photographic diary* covering one week of their school, home, and social life. Using low-cost disposable cameras, they will be asked to focus on critical incidents related to their experience of smoking cessation. Subsequently, photographs from the photo diary will be discussed during *recorded interviews*.

> **Comment:** The first three paragraphs spell out what data will be produced and how they will be collected.

Quantitative data from the questionnaire survey will be analysed using basic descriptive statistics looking at prevalence rates for smoking cessation and exploring their association with other relevant variables. Qualitative data from the focus group transcripts will be analysed using both content analysis and discourse analysis. Photographic diaries and the interviews will be interpreted using narrative analysis.

> **Comment:** The data analysis techniques are outlined here.

The research will be conducted during a 12-month period starting October 20xx and the data collection phase of the research will take place during a 6-month period starting in February 20xy. Authorization for the research has been obtained from both the local education authorities in the region, and head teachers at all secondary schools in these local education authorities have been contacted seeking agreement in principle to participate in the study.

> **Comment:** Duration of the research is specified, and the issue of access to the data sites is broached.

Methods

The research will use a sequential QUAN-QUAL research design (Creswell 2009). The use of a mixed methods approach is appropriate in relation to the research questions which require the measurement of factual information about the extent of smoking cessation within the specific age group as well as an understanding of the way people in this age group feel about smoking and its significance for their lives. As Johnson et al. (2007) stress, it is important that a mixed methods design brings the quantitative and the qualitative elements together so that they feed into each other and, in the

> **Comment:** Refers to key writers in relation to the chosen research strategy.

proposed research, this is evident in the way the findings from the survey will be used to provide stimulus material for the subsequent focus groups.

The mixed methods approach allows the research to build on the strengths and compensate for the weaknesses inherent in the different strategies and methods that will be used. The questionnaire survey will provide a foundation of quantitative data derived from a representative sample of young people aged 15–16 years. In terms of external validity, the findings can be checked against indicators from national statistics for smoking among young people (Fuller 2011). The findings will also be subject to member validation in the sense that they will be reported to the focus groups, the members of which will be invited to comment on the face validity of the data. The qualitative research will provide the kind of depth and insight that cannot be obtained through a questionnaire survey, although, in their case, the depth of information they provide will be based on a relatively small, purposively selected sample.

> **Comment:** Makes a case for why the strategy and methods are appropriate for the research.

The use of descriptive statistics and the analysis of text data using content, discourse, and narrative analysis is appropriate because the proposed research is exploratory in nature. Although theories of health-related behaviour do exist, they do not yet provide the foundation to allow the use of an explanatory research design that could be used to investigate the causal relationship between specific variables.

> **Comment:** Justifies use of an exploratory approach to the topic.

Use of a web-based questionnaire has some distinct advantages over the use of paper-based questionnaires. There are no substantial differences in the completion rates or the quality of data obtained from the different modes of delivery (Denscombe 2006). Web-based questionnaires, however, are less expensive and are more efficient in terms of turnaround time and the data entry/checking process. The reliability of the data collection tool will be checked using a split-half technique (Cronbach's alpha). The administration of the questionnaire will be arranged with the cooperation of teachers at the collaborating schools. All pupils in Year 10 of the schools will be invited to complete the online questionnaire using the computer labs in the schools at pre-arranged sessions. The questionnaire will comprise 20 questions and take no more than 10 minutes to complete. Allowing for movement to and from the labs and for giving relevant instructions, each group of students will require approximately 30 minutes away from scheduled routine classes.

> **Comment:** Justifies the use of an online questionnaire and provides some detail about how the data will be collected.

The researcher is currently a member of teaching staff at one of the schools in the region in which the proposed research will be conducted. For the purposes of objectivity and impartiality this school will not be included in the sample.

> **Comment:** Acknowledges the role of the researcher and demonstrates a concern for objectivity.

Limitations

The research will be exploratory and its findings should not be regarded as exhaustive or universally applicable. The purposive sampling and small numbers that will be used in relation to the focus groups and the photographic diaries will limit the extent to which the findings from the qualitative research can be generalized to the wider population of 15–16-year-olds. And it should be borne in mind that the quantitative survey data will be based on a sample of young people from one particular region of England, which could affect the applicability of findings nationally and internationally.

> **Comment:** This sets boundaries around expectations about what the research can produce. Limits to generalizations are acknowledged.

The cross-sectional research design will provide a snapshot of the situation as it is at this point in time, but will not provide data that can track changes over time. Existing evidence suggests that smoking cessation is a process that often requires repeated attempts (DiClemente et al. 1991), and a follow-up study would be needed to check the longer-term success of those in the photographic diary part of the study in their efforts to quit smoking.

> **Comment:** Inherent limitation of the chosen research design is noted.

Resource constraints mean that the research will take place over a relatively limited time scale with data collection affected by school holidays and school exams. This will restrict the amount of data that can be collected and will limit the overall scope of the project. Resource constraints will also prevent following up non-participants to gauge whether there are significant differences between participants and those who choose not to take part in the study.

> **Comment:** Time and resources inevitably restrict what can be done.

8. Planning and resources

This small-scale project will be undertaken principally by one person. The researcher will draw on the voluntary cooperation of teachers in the schools to enable data

> **Comment:** Not a team of researchers; no salary implications.

collection. The researcher's qualified teacher status will help facilitate access to the schools and obtain the cooperation of colleagues teaching 15–16-year-old pupils in those schools. The research will be conducted on a part-time basis during the early months of the research (about 8 hours a week) with additional time becoming available during the data collection phase through agreed work release (allowing about 16 hours a week).

> **Comment:** This addresses both the researcher skills issue and the matter of gaining access to data sources.

> **Comment:** Information on the amount of time that will be dedicated to the research.

The main items of expenditure that will not be covered by institutional overheads total £500. These comprise:

> **Comment:** Items listed that are not subsumed elsewhere.

Travel: £250
- Two visits each to the 12 schools involved in the questionnaire survey: £150 (based on an average 30 miles return on each occasion).
- Four visits to each of the sub-sample of 4 schools involved in the focus groups and photographic diaries: £100 (based on an average 30 miles return on each occasion).

Questionnaire: £50 (based on 2 months web-based questionnaire using education rate provided by SurveyMonkey or Zoomerang).

Equipment: £100 (8 low-cost disposable cameras. Recording equipment for interviews is already available. There will be no costs associated with hosting the focus group meetings.)

The costs of specialist software for data analysis (SPSS, NVivo) will be covered by site licences available to the researcher through employment. Printing costs for producing the Final Report will be covered by the researcher's employer.

> **Comment:** This acknowledges that many of the costs of research are covered by organizations such as the employer or the university.

The planned schedule for the research takes account of the increased number of hours dedicated to the data collection phase and also accommodates the timing of school holidays and end-of-year exams (see chart opposite).

Oct–Dec 20xx		Jan–March 20xy			April–June 20xy		July–Sept 20xy	
Literature review	Refine research questions					Update literature review		
		Design and pilot the questionnaire		Plan focus groups and photo diaries				
	Negotiate access to data sources		Questionnaire survey		Focus groups; Photo diaries & interviews			
				Analyse survey data		Analyse qualitative data		
					Drafts of sections/chapters			Write final report

9. Ethics

The research involves primary data collection from individuals and therefore an application for ethics approval has been made to the Human Research Ethics Committee at Redforest University. Research activity will not start before this approval is obtained. A preliminary risk assessment has been undertaken involving experienced researchers and teaching professionals, and reasonable efforts have been made in the design of the research to avoid foreseeable risks of harm to participants or others involved in the research. The research will be conducted in accordance with the Social Research Association's code of research ethics (http://www.the-sra.org.uk/documents/pdfs/ethics03.pdf). Criminal Records Bureau (CRB) clearance has been obtained for the researcher.

> **Comment:** Ethics approval process has been started.

> **Comment:** Some informal risk assessment has taken place.

> **Comment:** The researcher commits to upholding good professional standards of conduct.

> **Comment:** Research involving young people needs to be careful about getting appropriate clearance.

Participation in the research will be entirely voluntary. Pupils will be informed, both verbally and in writing, that they are under no obligation to take part in the research and that they have the right to withdraw from involvement in the project at any time. They will be supplied in advance with information about the purpose of the research and who is conducting it. They will also be given guarantees of anonymity and assured that any information they provide will be treated in the strictest confidence (subject to the proviso that the researcher has an overriding legal obligation in relation to the disclosure of certain kinds of information). No inducements will be offered to encourage participation.

> **Comment:** This paragraph demonstrates an awareness of the key research ethics principles.

A written consent form explaining the nature of the research and their involvement in it will be given to all the relevant pupils: only those who sign this form will be included in the research. All parents of relevant pupils will also receive a copy of the consent form and will be asked to contact the school if they have any objections to their child's involvement in the research.

> **Comment:** This shows how the principles will be applied – particularly with respect to written consent. Parental approval is sought, reflecting the age-status of the 15–16-year-olds.

Data from the research will be kept secure and precautions taken to prevent the leaking of confidential information. Data files held on computer will be encrypted and protected by password access. Documents and other materials will be kept under lock and key. Data will be kept for 5 years following completion of the project.

> **Comment:** This explains how confidentiality and data security will be assured.

A research website will be constructed that will allow transparency of dealings with participants. The findings will be disseminated initially through the research website. Participants will be encouraged to access these and to provide feedback to the researcher via email. The research will be conducted under the auspices of Redforest University. The research is not funded by a sponsor, and there is no conflict of interest in relation to the objective and impartial treatment of the data.

> **Comment:** Transparency and fairness are confirmed as features of the researcher's approach.

10. Outcomes

The findings of the research will be produced in a Final Report. This report will contain insights and information gleaned from the research about smoking cessation and young people. It will also include rec-ommendations arising from the research in relation to health education and health promotion. A summary of the Final Report will be lodged with the local education authorities and the schools who took part in the research, who will be encouraged to implement the recommendations arising in relation to health

> **Comment:** This identifies a 'deliverable' – a substantial end-product to the research.

> **Comment:** This indicates some clear, practical suggestions from the research.

education in schools. A summary of the Final Report will also be sent to smoking cessation support services in the region with a view to discussing the implications of the research for their service provision. The findings and recommendations will be open access and available online via the research website.

> **Comment:** Dissemination of the findings is described, along with efforts to give the research some impact on policies and practices.

11. References

ASH (2011) *Smoking Statistics*. London: Action on Smoking and Health. Available at: http://www.ash.org.uk/information/facts-and-stats (accessed 1 March 2012).

Centers for Disease Control and Prevention (2009) High school students who tried to quit smoking cigarettes – United States, 2007. *Morbidity and Mortality Weekly Report*, 58(16): 428–431.

Clark, M.A., Kviz, F.J., Crittenden, K.S. and Warnecke, R.B. (1998) Psychosocial factors and smoking cessation behaviors among smokers who have and have not ever tried to quit. *Health Education Research*, 13(1): 145–153.

Creswell, J.W. (2009) *Research Design: Qualitative, Quantitative, and Mixed Methods Approaches* (3rd edn.). Thousand Oaks, CA: Sage.

Denscombe, M. (2006) Web-based questionnaires: an assessment of the mode effect on the validity of data. *Social Science Computer Review*, 24(2): 246–254.

Denscombe, M. (2010) The affect heuristic and perceptions of 'the young smoker' as a risk object. *Health, Risk and Society*, 12(5): 425–440.

Denscombe, M. and Drucquer, N. (1999) Critical incidents and invulnerability to risk: young people's experience of serious health-related incidents and their willingness to take health risks. *Health, Risk and Society*, 1(2): 195–207.

DiClemente, C.C., Prochaska, J.O., Fairhurst, S.K., Velicer, W.F., Velasquez, M.M. and Rossi, J.S. (1991) The process of smoking cessation: an analysis of precontemplation, contemplation and preparation stages of change. *Journal of Consulting and Clinical Psychology*, 39: 295–304.

Dozois, D.N., Miser, A. and Farrow, J.A. (1995) Smoking patterns and cessation motivations during adolescence. *International Journal of the Addictions*, 30(11): 1485–1498.

Fuller, E. (ed.) (2011) *Smoking, Drinking and Drug Use Among Young People in England in 2010*. London: NHS Information Centre.

Grimshaw, G. and Stanton, A. (2010) *Tobacco Cessation Interventions for Young People*. Cochrane Library 2010 Issue 1. London: Wiley.

Johnson, R.B., Onwuegbuzie, A.J. and Turner, L.A. (2007). Toward a definition of mixed methods research. *Journal of Mixed Methods Research*, 1(2): 112–133.

Social Research Association (2003) *Ethical Guidelines*. Available at: http://www.the-sra.org.uk/documents/pdfs/ethics03.pdf (accessed 13 February 2012).

Stanton, W.R., Ferry, D., Elwood, C. and McClelland, M. (1996a) Prevalence, reliability and bias of adolescents' reports of smoking and quitting. *Addiction*, 91(11): 1705–1714.

Stanton, W.R., Gillespie, A.M. and Lowe, J.B. (1996b) Adolescents' experiences of smoking cessation. *Drug and Alcohol Dependence*, 43(1/2): 63–70.

Sutton, S. (1994) Understanding smoking relapse: predisposing factors, precipitating factors, and a combined model, in G. Edwards and M. Lader (eds.) *Addiction: Processes of Change*. Oxford: Oxford University Press (pp. 111–127).

WHO (2006) *Tobacco: Deadly in Any Form or Disguise*. Geneva: World Health Organization.

Appendix 3

HEADINGS AND SECTIONS IN A RESEARCH PROPOSAL

The following list of contents comprises a generic format that can be used in relation to small-scale research projects in the social sciences. It provides a specimen list of headings and sections that will be applicable for proposals in subject areas such as social studies, business studies, market research, education, health studies, politics, policy studies, psychology, and other similar research that includes primary data collection involving people.

CONTENTS

1 Title x

2 Keywords x

3 Aims of the research x

4 Background/Literature review x

5 Research questions x

6 Data collection x

7 Research methods x

8 Planning and resources x

9 Research ethics x

10 Limitations x

11 Research outcomes x

12 List of references x

Such a list of headings and sections will be familiar to most people who evaluate research proposals. However, as stressed in Chapter 1, there is no such thing as a definitive, universally accepted structure for all research proposals. Bearing this in mind, it is useful to look at some alternative examples that have been suggested elsewhere. It is easy to see the family resemblance between these but, equally, it is interesting to note the subtle variations in emphasis for different disciplines and styles of research. In the examples below note how sometimes there is a difference in the order in which the sections are listed, and some differences too in the level of detail that is required, with some of the examples recommending the inclusion of appendices.

Social research proposals (Dawson 2009: 58–63)

1 Title
2 Background
3 Aims and objectives
4 Methodology/Methods
5 Timetable
6 Budget and resources
7 Dissemination

Social science research proposals (Punch 2006: 61)

1 Title and title page
2 Abstract
3 Introduction: area, topic, and statement of purpose
4 Research questions: (a) general, (b) specific
5 Conceptual framework, theory, hypotheses
6 The literature
7 Methods
   • Design: strategy and framework
   • Sample
   • Data collection: instruments and procedures
8 Data analysis
9 Significance
10 Limitations and delimitations
11 Ethical issues: consent, access, and participants' protection
12 References
13 Appendices

Notes

- In some types of research, the research questions come after the literature section.
- In some situations, sections on costs (budget), risk management, and timetables are required.
- A table of contents that appears immediately after the title page is helpful to readers.

Qualitative research proposals (Marshall and Rossman 1999: 24)

1 Introduction
  - Overview
  - Topic and purpose
  - Potential significance
  - Framework and general research questions
  - Limitations
2 Review of related literature
  - Theoretical traditions
  - Essays by informed experts
  - Related research
3 Design and methodology
  - Overall approach and rationale
  - Site or population selection
  - Data-gathering methods
  - Data analysis procedures
  - Trustworthiness
  - Personal biography
  - Ethical and political considerations
4 Appendices

Mixed methods research proposals (Creswell 2003: 53–54)

1 Introduction
  - Statement of the problem
  - Purpose of the study (include both qualitative and quantitative statements and a rationale for mixing methods)

- Research questions (include both qualitative and quantitative)
- Review of the literature (separate section, if quantitative)

2 Procedures or methods
  - Characteristics of mixed methods research
  - Type of mixed methods design (include decisions involved in its choice)
  - Visual model and procedures of the design
  - Data collection procedures (types of data, sampling strategy)
  - Data analysis and validity procedures
  - Report presentation structure

3 Role of the researcher
4 Potential ethical issues
5 Significance of the study
6 Preliminary pilot findings
7 Expected outcomes
8 Appendices: instruments or protocols, outline for chapters, and proposed budget

Social science proposals (Kumar 2005: 188–189)

1 An introduction, including a brief literature review
2 Theoretical framework that underpins your study
3 Conceptual framework that constitutes the basis of your study
4 Objectives or research questions of your study
5 Hypotheses to be tested, if applicable
6 Study design that you are proposing to adopt
7 Setting for your study
8 Research instrument(s) you are planning to use
9 Sampling design and sample size
10 Ethical issues involved and how you propose to deal with them
11 Data processing procedures
12 Proposed chapters of the report
13 Problems and limitations of the study
14 Proposed time scale for the project

Proposals in behavioural sciences – including health/ medical research and psychological research
(Krathwohl and Smith 2005: 203–206)

1 Introductory material
  - Cover page
  - Title

- Abstract
- Table of contents
- Acknowledgements
2 Problem statement
  - General problem
  - Study focus
  - Study purpose
  - Study importance
  - Inquiry framework
  - Inquiry statement
  - Study boundaries
  - Terms
  - Summary
3 Literature review
  - Overview
  - Selection process
  - Review process
  - Literature quality
  - Major works
  - Substantive findings
  - Methodological findings
  - Implications
  - Contributions
  - Summary
4 Method statement
  - Research approach
  - Study design
  - Interventions/treatments
  - Data collection
  - Instrumentation
  - Data analysis
  - Work plan
  - Resources
  - Pilot studies
  - Limitations
5 Appendix
  - References
  - Bibliography
  - Dissertation outline
  - Sample instruments
  - Amplification of procedures
  - Copies of key documents
  - Institutional review board clearances (ethics)
  - Letters
  - Support requests
  - Résumé: student curriculum vitae

Science proposals (Friedland and Folt 2000: 35)

1 Project summary
2 Table of contents
3 Project description
4 Results from prior agency support
5 Statement of the problem and significance
6 Introduction and background
   • Relevant literature review
   • Preliminary data
   • Conceptual or empirical model
   • Justification of approach or novel methods
7 Research plan
   • Overview of research design
   • Objectives, hypotheses, and methods
   • Analysis and expected results
   • Timetable
8 References cited

Proposals for winning grant funding (Meador 1991: 20)

1 Cover letter
2 Title page
3 Table of contents
4 Proposal summary or Abstract
5 Introduction
6 Statement of the research problem
7 Objectives and expected benefits of the project
8 Description of the project
9 Timetable for the project
10 Key project participants
11 Project budget
12 Administrative provisions and organizational chart
13 Alternative funding
14 Post-project planning
15 Appendices and support materials
16 Bibliography and references

Note: The headings relating to participants, administration, and budgeting come to prominence in proposals aimed at attracting funding.

Appendix 4

CHOOSING A RESEARCH TOPIC

Top tip

Choose a good topic for research – it is important for the success of the proposal.

When it comes to choosing a research topic there are a variety of points from which people can start. Many people find themselves required to undertake a small-scale piece of research, perhaps a research project for a bachelor's or master's degree, without necessarily having in mind a topic they wish to investigate. Faced with the need to conduct a piece of research in a relatively short time and knowing that their work will be formally assessed, choosing a topic for research can pose quite a challenge. For such people the question is: 'How do I decide what topic to research?'

Top tip

Some initial questions to set the ball rolling:

What are my main interests?

Who am I and what principles do I stand for?

What things in my personal and academic background have shaped my beliefs?

Are there any assignments I have done that could be developed into a small-scale research project?

Many others start from a position where they have some rough idea of the kind of thing they would like to research but are not sure exactly what they want to research within that area. The challenge is to fine-tune their interest in a general area – to move it from something vague to something precise. For them the question is: 'How do I select a specific aspect of the topic?'

Top tip

Two ways to narrow the field of choice:

- Use review articles and systematic literature reviews in academic journals to provide signposts about which topics are being discussed and which writers to refer to.
- Look at the titles of projects and dissertations that have been done by students on the programme in previous years. Do not copy any of these, but do use them to get ideas about what kinds of topics would be suitable.

Then there are some who approach research with a very clear and definite vision of the topic they wish to investigate. Experienced researchers who are proposing a piece of research that builds on their previous work will have a clear project in mind, and applicants for a place on a PhD programme are likely to use their master's dissertation as the basis for selecting the subject matter for their research proposal. Practitioners working within an organization might have a specific work-related problem in mind that they wish to tackle. They know in advance what they want to achieve and they are likely to have a pretty good idea of what it will involve. And then there are those people who have a burning desire to investigate a particular topic that is of personal interest – something that ignites their concern or something that they just find fascinating. For such people, there is still a challenge to be faced. For them the question is: 'How do I justify my choice of topic?'

Top tip

The choice of topic must be justified to those who are to evaluate the proposal. Do not presume the readers will share your enthusiasm for your chosen topic. You need to sell them the idea – persuade them that you have made a good choice of topic.

This appendix is of relevance for all of these starting points. This is because it offers guidance that operates on the premise that a 'good' topic is one that can be 'sold' as an idea. What matters is not what the researcher thinks about the topic. The success of a proposal does not depend on how good the researcher believes the topic to be, but on how well it is justified to the audience of readers who will evaluate the proposal. It is the evaluators' opinions that ultimately count and, bearing in mind the points made in Chapters 2 and 3, this means that any topic that is 'good' must strike the evaluators as being:

- *relevant* (fitting with the remit for the research set by those to whom the proposal will be submitted);
- *worthwhile* (is necessary and offers suitable benefits);
- *feasible* (in terms of scope, available resources, access to data, researcher skills, ethics and legality).

A topic that meets the remit for the work

The vast majority of people who need to choose a topic for research will find that they are not entirely free in their choice. In practice, their choice of topic will need to fit in with the expectations of those who will evaluate the proposal – whether these are supervisors in university departments, representatives of funding bodies, or members of research ethics committees. Students will find that the range of topics from which they can choose will be restricted to those that fit in with the academic department within which they are studying, the programme on which they are enrolled, and possibly the course/module they are taking. Bachelor's degree projects and master's degree dissertations might allow some range of possibilities but they will include boundaries set by the academic discipline of the award for which the work is being produced. Similar restrictions apply in the case of PhD applications and funding applications where the topic that is chosen must fall within certain more or less explicit boundaries based on subject disciplines. So, for example, within a Business School, if a master's degree student proposed to conduct research on 'Styles of management and the success of Premier League sides', this might raise questions about how well it meets the remit for work within the discipline. There is, in effect, an ambiguity to this title. If it means that the research will look at the business side of running a club – finances, administration, organizational structure, human resources, etc. – then this is suitable. If, however, it is concerned with the coaching styles of football managers, it will fall outside the boundaries of what is appropriate for a Business School, and is better suited to a Sports Science Faculty.

> **Top tip**
>
> Ensure that your choice of topic fits well within the requirements of the academic programme, the sponsors, or funding body for whom the proposal is being written.

A topic that can be researched

A topic for research should be something that lends itself to being researched using methods that are conventional within the field of study. Basically, there are certain things that it is not feasible to study using conventional research methods and evaluators will want to know from the start that the questions posed are of a kind that research can answer. The questions need to be answerable in the sense that they rely on the collection and analysis of 'evidence' and on scientific debate and reason. The study cannot be something that relies on judgements or sentiments based on things like religious faith, moral beliefs, political ideology, artistic vision or metaphysics. Table A.1 provides an indication of the difference between those topics that lend themselves to being researched in a conventional sense and those that call for different modes of enquiry.

TABLE A.1 Topics that can and cannot be researched

Not researchable	Researchable
Should the UK become a republic? *[This requires a political judgement]*	What would be the constitutional changes needed to make the UK a republic? Is public opinion in favour of retaining the monarchy?
What is the best rock band in the world? *[This is based on an aesthetic judgement and/or emotional feeling]*	What criteria do people use when choosing the best rock band? What is the most popular rock band in the world based on annual earnings from record sales and live performances?
Is euthanasia a good thing? *[This calls for a moral judgement]*	Under what circumstances would members of the public support the practice of euthanasia?

A topic that is legal and ethical

In a free society there should be no topic which, in itself, is illegal to investigate. However, the act of investigating certain topics can easily put the researcher on the wrong side of the law. Research into topics such as terrorism, drug smuggling, people trafficking, prostitution, and child pornography illustrate the point. It is not against the law to research such topics, and indeed such research is potentially valuable for what it might disclose. And it does not mean that research on such topics must *inevitably* require the researcher to break the law. However, there is a real risk that any empirical research in such areas might end up breaking the law – intentionally or otherwise. Through the activities of gaining access to data sources, in the act of collecting the data, and even in the act of analysing the data, there is the danger of straying outside the bounds of what is within the law. Such topics should be avoided, then, bearing in mind that:

- researchers have no special exemption when it comes to compliance with the law and can be prosecuted if they break the law;
- no university or funding body will accept a research proposal that looks as though it will involve breaking the law.

Top tip

Play safe. Do not choose a topic that might lead you to break the law in the process of collecting or analysing data.

Research activity not only needs to be legal, it also needs to be ethical. When choosing a topic careful consideration should be given to whether it will be possible to adhere to a code of research ethics in the process of collecting and analysing the data and disseminating the findings from the research. Codes of research ethics are based on the principle that participants in research and others directly affected by the research should be treated with respect and that researchers should avoid causing harm as a consequence of their research activity. In practice, this means researchers are expected to:

- avoid undue intrusion – by minimizing inconvenience and taking care not to upset participants or cause them stress;
- protect the interests of participants – in particular, by preventing disclosure of identities, and maintaining the confidentiality of records;
- obtain informed consent from participants;
- avoid any misrepresentation or deception in their dealings with participants.

Top tip

Consider the consequences. When choosing a topic consider the ethical implications of doing the research, in particular the consequences of the research for the participants.

A focused topic with specific aims

The research topic needs to be fairly *specific*. A broad topic might be a good starting point, but it remains too wide-ranging and vague to be a viable focus for a small-scale project. It is vital to focus in on specific aspects, specific questions, specific issues within the broader area of interest. If this is not done, the readers of the proposal are likely to have doubts about (a) whether the ideas for research have been sufficiently developed, or (b) whether the researcher has failed to grasp the scale of the enterprise that is being proposed. Those who evaluate the proposal, as experienced researchers, will probably suspect that any effort to research such a broad area will prove to be unsuccessful because the researcher will inevitably:

- bite off more than he or she can chew;
- flounder in a sea of vast quantities of issues and data;
- waste time on the collection of unnecessary information
- waste time on meanderings up blind alleys before a clear direction becomes evident.

Link up with **Chapter 4: Aims of the Research**

Link up with **Delimitations and scoping the research**, p. 69

Link up with **Chapter 6: Research Questions**

Link up with **Chapter 8: Planning and Resources**

Restricting the scope of a topic can be fairly straightforward. In many cases, it is simply a matter of making explicit some of the assumptions surrounding the chosen topic. The location of the research, for instance, is often left unstated when it actually has a significant bearing on the nature of the proposed research and the applicability of its findings. As the findings from research become globally available through the Internet, it becomes increasingly important to appreciate the need to specify where the research will take place – which country/region, or which organization. The era under investigation, likewise, is easy to overlook when writing about the topic, even though it might actually be the intention of the researcher to focus on certain years as parameters for the research. In social research the age, sex, ethnicity,

FIGURE A.1 Narrowing the topic: an example

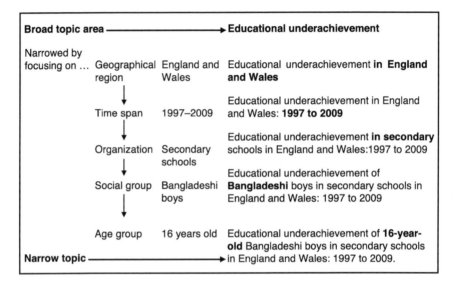

and social class of the people being studied are quite common ways in which the broad topic area is made more specific in terms of the actual topic for the proposed piece of research. Figure A.1 shows how this might look in practice.

Personal agenda and self-identity

There is one factor that influences the choice of topic for research that is generally underplayed when it comes to writing the proposal. That is the matter of the researcher's personal agenda and self-interest. In practice, though, this is a very significant factor because it has a bearing on the choice of topic in the large majority of cases.

Of interest to self – a means of personal development

In the first instance, people tend to choose topics that are of interest to themselves. This is quite reasonable when we consider the amount of time that will be spent on the research and the advantages of selecting a topic that can continue to motivate us during the hour upon hour of work that will go into the completion of the research. What we are interested in, of course, is affected by who we are and what we do.

Researcher's social identity – a reflection of personal background and experiences

Within the social sciences in particular, the choice of topic tends to reflect the personal identity and personal background of the researcher. The sex and ethnic background of the researcher, for instance, are likely to have a bearing on the choice of topic. Most research on gender inequality is conducted by women, whereas most research on race prejudice is conducted by ethnic minority researchers. This is no accident, and nor is it necessarily a bad thing. It does not automatically mean that the researcher is taking the easy route by choosing a topic in which they already have some insight, some experience, and some personal interest. On the contrary, it can often be the case that the personal attributes of the researcher can be a positive benefit for the proposed research – qualities that rather than being shunned as subjective and unscientific in relation to the choice of topic should be appreciated as important ingredients for the success of a project

Professional self-interest – a means of career advancement

Self-interest can play a role in the choice of topic such as when people select topics that they can see will have some personal benefit in terms of their employment. The choice of topic can be a strategic one. In the work setting employees can choose a topic mindful of the fact that their research on the topic can provide a practical solution or some other kind of pay-off that can serve them well in their career. The research might, for example, be the basis of a report that will impress the boss.

Interest, involvement, and bias

Self-interest in a topic is no bad thing in its own right. However, there are times when it can become an impediment to good research. A passionate interest in a topic can threaten the prospects of producing an impartial, objective piece of work. The passion felt for the topic might come to stand in the way of the ability to approach the topic in an unbiased manner. The questions the researcher needs to ask are:

- Do I have a vested interest in the findings from the research?
- Will I be able to approach the topic with an open mind?
- Could I incorporate ideas and views I passionately disagree with and be willing and able to consider both sides of the argument?
- Am I too close to the subject, too involved?
- Will my personal values, beliefs, and background lead to biased findings?

- What chance is there that my research will provide a fair and balanced picture?

Caution! Justifying the choice of topic

There is an important point to bear in mind when it comes to justifying the selection of a research topic. In the context of a research proposal, the personal and practical reasons for choosing a particular topic will *not*, of themselves, persuade the readers that the research is worthwhile. In most disciplines, the prevailing sentiment is that research topics should be justified in relation to theoretical developments in the field or practical problems that need a remedy. They are not justified on the basis that the researcher had a personal interest in the topic or that the topic was nice and convenient to study. Although in practice the personal interests of the researcher and the convenience of the topic might have a strong influence on the choice of topic, when justifying the choice of topic in the context of the research proposal the emphasis should be placed firmly on the potential benefits of the research for the likes of theory, knowledge, and practice in the subject area.

The proposal, then, needs to argue a case that there is a need for the particular investigation because, in ways described within the proposal, the research will do one or more of the following:

- fill a gap in what is already known about the topic, perhaps by adding some useful information or by applying current theories and methods in new contexts;
- examine some contradictions that currently exist within theories or data on the topic;
- contribute to a debate or controversy around the topic;
- provide a timely commentary on some significant contemporary issue;
- examine a practical problem, with a view to providing a remedy;
- produce guidelines for good practice.

> **Top tip**
> When it comes to justifying a topic for research:
>
> - the way the topic fits with existing research knowledge can be used to persuade the readers that the topic is *worthwhile*;
> - the way the topic fits with personal identity and researcher background can be used to persuade the readers of the *feasibility* of the project.

References

Allen, E.M. (1960) Why are research grant applications disapproved?, *Science*, 132(3439), 1532–4.

Andrews, R. (2003) *Research Questions*. London: Continuum.

Aronson, E. (1999) *The Social Animal*. New York: Worth.

Belmont Report (1979) *Ethical Principles and Guidelines for the Protection of Human Subjects of Research: Report of the National Commission for the Protection of Human Subjects of Biomedical and Behavioral Research*. Washington, DC: Department of Health, Education and Welfare.

Bryman, A. (2007) The research question in social research: what is its role?, *International Journal of Social Research Methodology*, 10(1), 5–20.

Campbell, J.P., Daft, R.L. and Hulin, C.L. (1982) *What to Study: Generating and Developing Research Questions*. Beverly Hills, CA: Sage.

Cialdini, R. (2007) *Influence: The Psychology of Persuasion*. New York: Collins.

Clark, L. (1987) *Identifying and Defining Questions for Research*. London: Distance Learning Centre, South Bank Polytechnic.

Creswell, J.W. (2003) *Research Design: Qualitative, Quantitative, and Mixed Methods Approaches* (2nd edn.). Thousand Oaks, CA: Sage.

Creswell, J.W. (2009) *Research Design: Qualitative, Quantitative, and Mixed Methods Approaches* (3rd edn.). Thousand Oaks, CA: Sage.

Cuca, J. and McLoughlin, W. (1987) Why clinical research grant applications fare poorly in review and how to recover, *Cancer Investigation*, 5(1), 55–8.

Dawson, C. (2009) *Introduction to Research Methods: A Practical Guide for Anyone Undertaking a Research Project* (4th edn.). Oxford: How To Books.

Denicolo, P. and Becker, L. (2012) *Developing Research Proposals (Success in Research)*. London: Sage.

Denscombe, M. (2005) Research ethics and the governance of research projects: the potential of Internet home pages, *Sociological Research Online*, 10(3). Available at: http://www.socresonline.org.uk/10/3/denscombe.html.

Denscombe, M. (2010) *Ground Rules for Social Research* (2nd edn.). Maidenhead: Open University Press.

Economic and Social Research Council (2010) *Framework for Research Ethics*. Swindon: ESRC. Available at: http://www.esrc.ac.uk/_images/Framework_for_Research_ Ethics_ tcm8-4586.pdf

Economic and Social Research Council (undated) *Impact Assessment*. Swindon: ESRC. Available at: http://www.esrc.ac.uk/impacts-and-findings/impact-assessment/.

Feyerabend, P. (1993) *Against Method: Outline of an Anarchistic Theory of Knowledge*. London: Verso (first published 1970).

Fink, A. (2010) *Conducting Research Literature Reviews: From the Internet to Paper* (3rd edn.). Thousand Oaks, CA: Sage.

Fraenkel, J., Wallen, N. and Hyun, H. (2011) *How to Design and Evaluate Research in Education* (6th edn.). New York: McGraw-Hill.

Friedland, A.J. and Folt, C.L. (2000) *Writing Successful Science Proposals*. New Haven, CT: Yale University Press.

Gerrish, K. and Lacey, A. (2010) Disseminating research findings, in K. Gerrish and A. Lacey (eds.) *The Research Process in Nursing* (6th edn.). Chichester: Wiley-Blackwell.

Gorard, S. (2003) *Quantitative Methods in Social Science*. London: Continuum.

Green, J. and Browne, J. (2005) Framing a research question, in J. Green and J. Browne (eds.) *Principles of Social Research*. Maidenhead: Open University Press.

Hart, C. (1998) *Doing a Literature Review: Releasing the Social Science Research Imagination*. London: Sage.

Hatton, A. (2007) *The Definitive Business Pitch*. Harlow: Pearson.

Hughes, C. (ed.) (2003) *Disseminating Qualitative Research in Educational Settings: A Critical Introduction*. Maidenhead: Open University Press.

Israel, M. and Hay, I. (2006) *Research Ethics for Social Scientists: Between Ethical Conduct and Regulatory Compliance*. London: Sage.

Krathwohl, D.R. and Smith, N.L. (2005) *How to Prepare a Dissertation Proposal: Suggestions for Students in Education and the Social and Behavioral Sciences*. Syracuse, NY: Syracuse University Press.

Kuhnke, E. (2012) *Persuasion and Influence*. Chichester: Wiley.

Kumar, R. (2005) *Research Methodology: A Step-by-Step Guide for Beginners* (2nd edn.). London: Sage.

Kumar, R. (2010) *Research Methodology: A Step-by-Step Guide for Beginners* (3rd edn.). London: Sage.

Leedy, P.D. and Ormrod, J.E. (2004) *Practical Research: Planning and Design* (8th edn.). Upper Saddle River, NJ: Prentice-Hall.

Leedy, P.D. and Ormrod, J.E. (2009) *Practical Research: Planning and Design* (9th edn.). Upper Saddle River, NJ: Prentice-Hall.

Lewis, I. and Munn, P. (2004) *So You Want to Do Research! A Guide for Beginners on How to Formulate Research Questions*. Glasgow: Scottish Council for Research in Education.

Locke, L.F., Spirduso, W.W. and Silverman, S.J. (2000) *Proposals that Work: A Guide for Planning Dissertations and Grant Proposals* (4th edn.). Thousand Oaks, CA: Sage.

Locke, L.F., Spirduso, W.W. and Silverman, S.J. (2007) *Proposals that Work: A Guide for Planning Dissertations and Grant Proposals* (5th edn.). Thousand Oaks, CA: Sage.

Lyons Morris, L. and Taylor Fitz-Gibbon, C. (1978) *How to Deal with Goals and Objectives*. Beverly Hills, CA: Sage.

Machi, L.A. and McEvoy, B.T. (2009) *The Literature Review: Six Steps to Success*. Thousand Oaks, CA: Corwin Press.

Marshall, C. and Rossman, G. (1999) *Designing Qualitative Research* (3rd edn.). Thousand Oaks, CA: Sage.

Marshall, C. and Rossman, G. (2006) *Designing Qualitative Research* (4th edn.). Thousand Oaks, CA: Sage.

Marshall, C. and Rossman, G. (2011) *Designing Qualitative Research* (5th edn.). Thousand Oaks, CA: Sage.

Mason, J. (2002) *Qualitative Researching*. London: Sage.

Ogden, T.E. and Goldberg, I.A. (2002) *Research Proposals: A Guide to Success* (3rd edn.). San Diego, CA: Academic Press.

Oliver, P. (2010) *The Student's Guide to Research Ethics* (2nd edn.). Maidenhead: Open University Press.

Punch, K. (2006) *Developing Effective Research Proposals* (2nd edn.). Thousand Oaks, CA: Sage.

Remenyi, D., Swan, N. and Van Den Assem, B. (2011) *Ethics Protocols and Research Ethics Committees*. Reading: Academic Publishing International.

Research Councils UK (undated) *Maximising Research Impact.* Swindon: RCUK. Available at: http://www.rcuk.ac.uk/kei/maximising/Pages/home.aspx.

Ridley, D.D. (2008) *The Literature Review: A Step-by-Step Guide for Students.* London: Sage.

Wallace, M. and Wray, A. (2011) *Critical Reading and Writing for Postgraduates* (2nd edn.). London: Sage.

Walliman, N. (2005) *Your Research Project: A Step-by-Step Guide for the First-time Researcher.* London: Sage.

White, P. (2009) *Developing Research Questions: A Guide for Social Scientists.* Basingstoke: Palgrave Macmillan.

Index

access to data 1, 20, 21, 24, 31, 60, 97,
98, 100, 101, 104, 106, 108, 118,
123, 131, 134, 144, 145, 151, 154,
155, 159, 166, 168
aims of research 1, 7, 9, 14, 20, 26, 41,
45–56, 62, 72–77, 82–84, 88–92,
102, 113, 119, 147–150, 158, 159,
169
Allen, E.M. 24, 173
analysis of data 19, 68, 74, 79, 94,
99–101, 106, 107, 117–120, 145,
151, 152, 154, 159–163
Andrews, R. 90, 173
Aronson, E. 42, 173
audience for proposals 7, 26, 32,
33–39, 41, 141, 166
evaluators 11–37, 41, 55, 89, 97, 105,
110, 111, 117, 119, 121, 124, 132,
133, 138, 141, 142, 166, 167

bachelor degree projects 2, 11, 12,
21–28, 57, 67, 68, 103, 110, 113,
115, 120, 140, 141, 164, 166
background to the research 9, 45, 46,
50–55, 84, 95, 147, 148, 158, 159,
163
Becker, L. 120, 173
Belmont Report 130, 173
benefits from research 1, 8, 9, 11, 17,
18, 28–36, 40, 53, 62, 65, 82, 127,
137, 145, 163, 166, 172
deliverables 8, 18, 138, 156
wider application 28, 31
particular interest 24–28, 32–37, 41,
51, 83, 84, 143, 164–172
Browne, J. 174
Bryman, A. 73, 173

Campbell, J.P. 90, 173
Cialdini, R. 42, 173

Clark, L. 79, 80, 149, 157, 173
communication of ideas 13, 35, 40, 41,
101, 118, 135, 141
clarity 35, 46, 55, 68, 76, 77, 82, 140
contents of proposals 15, 35, 47, 48,
54, 70, 147, 158–163
costs of research 8, 9, 21, 24, 97, 109,
110, 113–117, 120, 138, 144, 145,
151, 154, 158–163
Creswell, J.W. 55, 79, 87, 90, 151, 157,
160, 173
Cuca, J. 24, 173

Daft, R.L 90, 173
Dawson, C. 108, 159, 173
definition of terms 30, 31, 49, 68, 71
delimitations 50, 56, 69–71, 87, 106,
159, 169
Denicolo, P. 120, 173
Denscombe, M. 26, 68, 120, 141, 149,
152, 157, 173
distinctive proposals 16, 25, 31, 39, 77

Economic and Social Research Council
13, 34, 38, 124, 126, 136, 143, 173
empirical data 2, 69, 70, 73, 80, 163, 168
ethics 1, 8, 9, 11, 12, 22, 31, 39, 47,
107, 121–136, 139, 142, 145, 147,
155–168
approval 10–12, 39, 47, 121, 122,
127, 132–135, 155
codes of 121, 125–128, 133, 135,
155, 168
principles 8, 22, 121, 126–131,
133–136, 156, 168
evaluation of the proposal 5, 7, 10–31,
34–37, 41, 47–63, 70–74, 86–90,
95–111, 117, 119, 121–124,
132–138, 141–143, 159, 165–169,
173

feasibility of research 1, 2, 7, 8, 16,
    19–22, 29–31, 41, 46, 55, 58, 92, 96,
    110, 117–119, 145, 166, 167, 172
Feyerabend, P. 17, 173
findings 7, 12, 18, 19, 28–31, 53,
    57–66, 74, 77, 80, 81, 86, 103–106,
    113, 122–125, 129–145, 149–157,
    161, 162, 168–171
    dissemination of 18, 125, 131, 137,
    141–143, 156, 157, 159, 168
    impact of 18, 137, 142, 143, 145,
    157
Fink, A. 71, 173
Folt, C. L. 120, 163, 174
Fraenkel, J. 31, 90, 173
Friedland, A. J. 163, 174

Gantt chart 21, 111, 119
Gerrish, K. 143, 174
Goldberg, I. 31, 174
Gorard, S. 82, 174
Green, J. 174

Hart, C. 71, 174
Hatton, A. 42, 174
Hay, I. 136, 174
headings 9, 10, 18, 69, 97, 158–163
Hughes, C. 143, 174
Hulin, C.L. 90, 173
Hyun, H. 31, 90, 173

Israel, M. 136, 174
iterative process 24, 56, 65, 70, 83,
    84

keywords 9, 45, 46, 48, 49, 54, 60, 61,
    147, 148, 158
Krathwohl, D. R. 15, 108, 161, 174
Kumar, R. 90, 161, 174
Kuhnke, E. 42, 174

Lacey, A. 143, 174
Leedy, P. 24, 31, 82, 174
legal research 1, 8, 22, 31, 52, 59, 98,
    115, 123, 128, 130, 131, 136, 145,
    156, 166–168
Lewis, I. 74, 174
limitations 38, 42, 69, 88, 91, 105–108,
    111, 113, 145, 153, 158–162, 169

literature review 7, 9, 17, 26, 30, 50,
    53, 56–71, 73–76, 84, 87, 89, 100,
    145, 147, 149, 155, 158–163, 165
    critique 26, 28, 50, 63, 64, 66, 70
    search 56, 59–62, 70
    selection 58162
Locke, L., 10, 15, 35, 80, 120, 174
Lyons Morris, L. 55, 174

Machi, L. 71, 174
Marshall, C. 55, 87, 108, 160, 174
Mason, J. 79, 174
masters degree dissertations 2, 11, 12,
    21, 24–28, 57, 58, 67, 68, 103, 110,
    113, 115, 120, 140, 141, 164–166
McEvoy, B. 71, 174
McLoughlin, W. 24, 173
Munn, P. 74, 174

Ogden, T. 31, 174
Oliver, P. 136, 174
open-minded approach 64, 72, 77, 86,
    90, 130, 136, 139, 171
originality of research 25–27, 31, 67,
    68, 70, 145
Ormrod, J. 24, 31, 82, 174
outcomes from research 8, 9, 11,
    18–20, 50, 65, 80, 90, 122,
    137–143, 145, 147, 150, 156, 158,
    161

persuasion 32–38, 42
Phd theses 2, 11, 12, 21, 24, 25,
    27, 31, 35, 36, 39, 57, 58, 67,
    103, 110, 113, 120, 140, 141, 143,
    165, 166
plagiarism 26, 68, 130, 145
planning 5, 6, 9, 14, 20, 21, 29,
    31, 50, 69, 89, 109–120, 139,
    147, 153, 158, 161, 163, 169
precision 7, 8, 17, 29–31, 34, 35, 46,
    47, 54, 68, 71, 73–79, 89, 94, 95,
    107, 145, 165
Punch, K. 15, 108, 159, 174

Remenyi, D. 132, 136, 174
Research Councils UK. 143, 175
research hypotheses 30, 73, 76, 78–8
    86–89, 139, 159, 161, 163

research methods 2, 7–9, 19, 21, 24, 26,
30, 46, 48, 54, 62, 64, 67–69, 75,
87, 91–108, 123–125, 129, 131, 136,
147, 150–152, 158–163, 167, 172
description of 8, 24, 91, 92, 94, 99,
101, 107
justification of 50, 69, 70, 91–93,
101–103, 107, 123, 127, 134, 136,
152, 163
exploratory research 78, 86, 87, 100,
102, 152, 153
grounded theory 86, 87, 93
qualitative 75, 76, 79, 86, 87, 89, 94,
95, 99–101, 103, 118, 150–155,
160, 161
quantitative 75, 76, 79, 89, 94, 99,
100, 101, 103, 118, 150–153, 160,
161
variables 75, 79
research proposals
as advertisements 32–41
approval of 5, 10–15, 29, 31, 33,
39, 41, 47, 57, 86, 100, 101, 115,
121–123, 127, 132, 133, 135,
155, 156
rejection 13–16, 23–25, 29, 122
submission process 5, 9, 12–15, 24,
25, 31, 36, 41, 115, 132, 144, 145
imeliness 26, 27, 31, 32, 36
nique selling points 32, 39
rch propositions 73, 76, 78, 81,
t, 86–90
h questions 8, 9, 19, 30, 54,
58, 70, 72–90, 93, 101, 103,
147, 149–151, 155, 158–161,

kills 22, 27, 49, 63, 69, 98,
, 119, 129, 134, 144, 154,

7–9, 16, 20, 21, 24, 25,
88, 100, 106, 109–120,
7, 153, 158, 159, 162,

20, 21, 25, 31, 33,
119, 137, 138
16–25, 31, 46,
74, 88, 102,

106–119, 128, 129, 138, 141, 144,
145, 153, 154, 159–163, 169, 170
Rossman, G. 55, 87, 108, 160, 174
Ridley, D. 71, 175
risk assessment 22, 31, 91, 103, 104,
107, 121, 131, 135, 144, 145, 155

sales pitch 32, 35, 39–42
scope of research 20, 21, 31, 47, 50, 55,
82, 94, 105, 108, 113, 117, 153,
166, 169,
selling an idea 1, 32–42, 46, 54, 65, 70,
165
small-scale projects 2, 17, 96, 103,
114–116, 153, 158, 164, 169
Silverman, S. 15, 120, 174
Smith, N. L. 15, 108, 161, 174
Spirduso, W. 15, 120, 174
success 1, 2, 5, 7, 8, 10, 11, 14, 15,
16–31, 35–41, 47, 53, 54, 73, 74,
86, 89, 98, 102, 118, 136, 143, 164,
166
Swan, N. 136, 174

Taylor Fitz-Gibbon, C. 55, 174
title 9, 45–49, 54, 147, 148, 158–163,
165, 166
topic 7, 17, 19, 20, 26–29, 33, 36,
50, 53, 56–70, 73, 76–81, 86–89,
102, 116–118, 123, 125, 131,
133, 139, 144, 145, 152, 159,
160, 164–172
truth 32, 38, 64

value for money 18, 137, 138
Van Den Assem, B. 136, 174

Wallace, M. 63, 175
Wallen, N. 31, 90, 173
Walliman, N. 108, 175
White, P. 78, 79, 82, 90, 175
worthwhile research 1, 2, 7, 8, 12,
16–31, 35, 39, 41, 46, 50, 55, 58,
65, 67, 68, 70, 88, 92, 105, 114,
116, 138, 141, 143, 148, 150, 166,
172
Wray, A. 63, 175